The FIRST 100 JAPANESE KANJI

The quick and easy way to learn the basic Japanese kanji

Introduction by
Eriko Sato

TUTTLE Publishing

Tokyo | Rutland, Vermont | Singapore

Published by Tuttle Publishing, an imprint of Periplus Editions (HK) Ltd.

www.tuttlepublishing.com

Copyright © 2008 by Periplus Editions (HK) Ltd.

ISBN: 978-4-8053-1008-3

Distributed by:

North America, Latin America & Europe
Tuttle Publishing
364 Innovation Drive
North Clarendon, VT 05759-9436 U.S.A.
Tel: 1 (802) 773-8930
Fax: 1 (802) 773-6993
info@tuttlepublishing.com
www.tuttlepublishing.com

Japan
Tuttle Publishing
Yaekari Building, 3rd Floor
5-4-12 Osaki
Shinagawa-ku
Tokyo 141 0032
Tel: (81) 3 5437-0171
Fax: (81) 3 5437-0755
www.tuttle.co.jp

Asia Pacific
Berkeley Books Pte. Ltd.
61 Tai Seng Avenue #02-12
Singapore 534167
Tel: (65) 6280-1330
Fax: (65) 6280-6290
inquiries@periplus.com.sg
www.periplus.com

First edition
13 12 11 10
10 9 8 7 6 5 4 3

Printed in Singapore

Contents

Introduction

Modern Japanese can be written horizontally, from left to right, or vertically, from top to bottom. Japanese is one of the rare languages that uses multiple writing systems simultaneously, sometimes even in the same sentence. It is written by combining Chinese characters, called *kanji*, and two sets of syllabic alphabets called *kana* (*hiragana* and *katakana*) along with a few punctuation marks. Each kanji character represents a meaning, while each kana character represents a sound. For example, the following short sentence contains kanji, hiragana, and katakana:

パーティーに来ました。
Pātī ni kimashita.
(He) came to the party.

The non-Chinese loanword パーティー, written **pātī** in Roman letters and meaning *party*, is written in katakana. The stem of the verb 来, pronounced *ki* and meaning *to come*, is written using kanji. The grammatical particle に, written **ni** in Roman letters and meaning *to*, and the inflectional element ました, pronounced **mashita** (polite past affirmative), are written in hiragana. Isn't it interesting that all three writing systems can be used in such a simple sentence?

The total number of kana is relatively small: there are only 46 basic characters for each kana system in modern Japanese. By contrast, the total number of kanji is quite large. The Japanese government selected a total of 1,945 kanji (the so-called **jōyō** kanji, or kanji for daily use) in 1981. Japanese students are expected to learn how to read all of these kanji by the time they graduate high school. Additional kanji are used in proper names and certain other words.

You might think that there are too many kanji characters to learn, but don't get discouraged! If you learn the first several hundred kanji characters, you will be able to understand or guess the meaning of most street signs, restaurant menus, merchandise names, a variety of instructions, and much more! Furthermore, it is a lot of fun to learn kanji because the characters have interesting historical and cultural backgrounds and amazing compositional structures. Each kanji character has a unique meaning and shape, so each time you learn a new kanji character, you'll feel a bit like you've made a new friend.

The key to your ultimate success is to learn the very first 100 kanji correctly and solidly. Then, the next 100 kanji can be more easily learned than the first 100, and the third 100 kanji can be learned even more easily than the second 100. You can see how important it is to start in the right way. Welcome to *The First 100 Japanese Kanji*! If you make a manageable plan for learning with this workbook everyday, you'll be able to enjoy the process of learning kanji and greatly improve your reading proficiency in Japanese. This introduction provides you with the basic information you need to know about the development and use of kanji and shows you how to write them properly.

How did kanji develop?

The word **kanji** literally means "characters of the Han Dynasty of ancient China" (206 B.C.E. to 220 A.D.). The initial forms of kanji originated in the Yellow River region of China between 2000 and 1500 B.C.E. The earliest preserved characters were written on tortoise shells and animal bones, and about 3,000 characters have been discovered from this early period. Depending on how they were formed, kanji can be classified into four main categories: pictorial kanji, indicative kanji, compound ideographic kanji, and phonetic-ideographic kanji.

Pictorial kanji originated from pictures of objects or phenomena. For example:

Meaning	Original Picture	Modern Kanji
River		川
Mountain		山
Tree		木
Sun		日
Moon		月
Rain		雨

Indicative kanji were created as symbolic representations of abstract concepts using points and lines. For example:

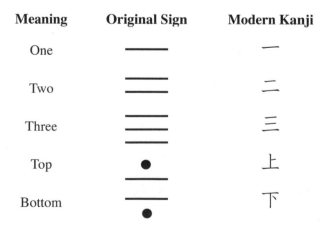

Meaning	Original Sign	Modern Kanji
One		一
Two		二
Three		三
Top		上
Bottom		下

Compound ideographic kanji were formed by combining two or more pictorial or indicative kanji to bring out a new but simple idea. For example:

Meaning	Combining Multiple Kanji	Resulting Kanji
Woods	木 + 木 tree + tree	林
Forest	木 + 木 + 木 tree + tree + tree	森
Bright	日 + 月 sun + moon	明

Finally, *phonetic-ideographic kanji* were formed by combining an element that expressed meaning and an element that carried the sound. For example, the following characters all stand for some body of water:

Meaning	Combining Elements	Kanji
Inlet	氵 + 工 *water* + KŌ	江
Ocean	氵 + 羊 *water* + YŌ	洋
River	氵 + 可 *water* + KA	河

The left side of each character above, 氵, contributes the meaning, showing that each kanji's meaning is related to water. The right side of each character, 工, 羊, or 可, contributes the sound, showing how the kanji should be pronounced.

Kanji characters were brought to Japan from China between the fourth and the fifth centuries A.D. Until then, there were no written symbols in Japanese. The Japanese initially developed a hybrid system where kanji were given Japanese pronunciations and were used for writing Japanese. This system proved unwieldy, since Japanese and Chinese grammar and structure are so different. Then, they developed a system, **man'yōgana**, in which a limited set of kanji was used to write Japanese words with their sounds. Hiragana and katakana were developed in the Heian Period (794-1185) from some of the kanji characters included in **man'yōgana**. About 2,000 kanji as well as hiragana and katakana are still used in modern Japanese. Interestingly, there are some kanji characters that were created in Japan. For example, the kanji 峠 (mountain pass), 畑 (field of crops), and 働 (work) were all created in Japan by combining multiple existing kanji components.

How are kanji pronounced?

The Japanese language is very different from the Chinese language, having very distinct grammar and sounds. Many Chinese words consist of one syllable, but most Japanese words have more than one syllable. So, the assignment of a Japanese pronunciation to each kanji required both flexibility and creativity.

On-readings and kun-readings

There are two different ways of reading kanji in Japanese: on-readings (or **on-yomi**) and kun-readings (or **kun-yomi**). When kanji characters were first introduced to Japan, the original Chinese pronunciations were also adapted with only minor modifications. Such Chinese ways of reading kanji are called on-readings and are still used, especially when a character appears as a part of a compound where two or more kanji are combined to form a word.

At the same time, many kanji characters were assigned the pronunciation of the existing native Japanese word whose meaning was closest to that of the character. Such Japanese readings are called kun-readings, and are used especially when a character occurs independently in a sentence. For example, the character 母 is pronounced **bo** (on-reading) when used as a part of the compound word 母国, **bokoku** (mother country), but is pronounced **haha** (kun-reading) when used by itself. This is illustrated in the following sentence.

私の母の母国はフランスです。
Watashi no haha no bokoku wa Furansu desu.
My mother's mother country is France.

In this workbook, on-readings are shown in katakana and, when Romanized, in upper-case letters. Conversely, kun-readings are shown in hiragana and in lower-case letters when Romanized.

Some kanji characters have more than one on-reading or kun-reading, and different readings are used in different contexts. Also note that there are special cases where it is not possible to clearly divide a kanji compound into components that can be pronounced separately.

Okurigana

As noted above, many Chinese words consist of a single syllable, expressed by only one Chinese character, but the corresponding Japanese words often have more than one syllable. In order to use kanji in the Japanese language, some kanji characters needed to be accompanied by kana. Such kana are called **okurigana**. Okurigana are particularly important for verbs and adjectives, which need inflectional elements, although they may also be used for other types of words, including nouns and adverbs. For example, in the following words, the kanji 高, meaning *expensive* or *high*, and the kana that follow jointly represent the pronunciation of the whole word, successfully representing its complete meaning:

高い	**takai**	expensive (plain present affirmative)
高くない	**takakunai**	not expensive (plain present negative)
高かった	**takakatta**	was expensive (plain past affirmative)

In this book, the okurigana are preceded by "–" when first presented in kun-readings.

Furigana
Kanji characters are occasionally provided with kana that shows how they are intended to be read in the given context. Such kana used as a pronunciation guide are called **furigana**. For example, the hiragana characters placed right above the kanji in the following word are furigana:

たか
高い

Furigana is often used for children or learners of Japanese. This can be a great help for you at the beginning! It is also used in newspapers for unusual readings and for characters not included in the officially recognized set of essential kanji. Japanese comic books use furigana generously!

How are kanji used in compounds?
Some Japanese words are represented by only one kanji (e.g., 赤, **aka**, *red*), but many Japanese words are represented by a kanji with okurigana (e.g., 高い, **takai**, *expensive*) or by a kanji compound. Kanji compounds constitute a large proportion of Japanese vocabulary. For example, 先生, written **sensei** in Roman letters, is a compound meaning *teacher*. It consists of two characters, 先 (ahead) and 生 (live). In general, on-readings are used for compounds, but occasionally, kun-readings are also used.

By the way, when you write a compound, there is no need to add a space between the kanji characters in it, but don't try to squeeze the characters together to fit in one-character space. Each character in a compound should take one-character space. For example, notice the difference between 女子(girl) and 好(to like). The first item (女子) is a kanji compound that consists of two kanji characters, 女 (woman) and 子(child). By contrast, the second item (好) is a single kanji character that consists of two kanji components, 女 and 子.

Some kanji compounds were created in Japan and have been brought back to China and are now being used there. Examples include 電話 **denwa** (telephone), 化学 **kagaku** (science), and 社会 **shakai** (society). Many kanji compounds are also used to represent Japanese culture, concepts, and ideas (e.g., 神道 **Shinto**) as well as to name Japanese people (e.g., 田中 **Tanaka**), institutions and companies (e.g., 三菱 **Mitsubishi**), places (e.g., 東京 **Tokyo**), and eras (e.g., 明治 **Meiji**). Regardless of their origin, kanji compounds form an essential part of the lives of Japanese people.

There are two special cases where you may have a hard time reading kanji compounds: **jukujikun** and **ateji**. A **jukujikun** is a unique kun-reading assigned to an entire kanji compound rather than to each kanji character separately. For example, the compound 明日 (tomorrow) can be read as **myōnichi** using the on-reading of each character in the compound one after another, as in the majority of typical kanji compounds, but can also be read as **asu**, which is a **jukujikun**. In the latter case, it is impossible to tell which syllable corresponds to 明 and which syllable corresponds to 日 because the reading is assigned to the whole compound. Other examples of **jukujikun** include 一日 **tsuitachi** (the first day of the month), 五月雨 **samidare** (early summer rain), 海老 **ebi** (shrimp), and 土産 **miyage** (souvenir).

Ateji are kanji characters whose sounds are used to represent native Japanese words or non-Chinese loanwords regardless of the meanings of the kanji. For example, the kanji compound 寿司 is made of **ateji**. It is pronounced **sushi**, and means sushi, the food, even though 寿 means *one's natural life span* and 司 means *to administer*, neither of which are directly related to food. Other examples of **ateji** include 目出度い **medetai** (happy), 出鱈目 **detarame** (random), and 珈琲 **kōhī** (coffee). Many **ateji** for non-Chinese loanwords, including proper names, have been replaced by katakana, but some are still used. In addition, new **ateji** are occasionally created.

What are radicals?
Most kanji characters are composed of two or more components. Each component may contribute to the kanji's meaning, sound, or merely its shape. For example, 日 is an independent kanji character meaning *sun*, but is also a component that lends meaning to many kanji. For example:

明 *bright*   時 *time*   晴 *clear up*

There are many kanji-components, but the most basic and identifiable elements of kanji are called *radicals*. For hundreds of years, Chinese dictionaries have organized kanji characters according to their radicals. Each Chinese characters was assigned a radical and placed in an appropriate section of a dictionary according to the designated radical.

It is not always clear which component of a kanji is the radical, but this workbook shows the radical for each kanji at the upper right corner of the page. Whenever you learn a new kanji using this book, check its radical. It will help you understand and remember the meaning and the internal composition of the kanji. Eventually, you will be able to identify the radical just by looking at a kanji. There is an index of characters organized by radical near the end of this book.

Depending on its position in a kanji character, radicals are classified into seven categories, as shown in the chart on the opposite page:

Name	Position		Example
偏 **hen** (lit., partial, one-sided)	left		イ にんべん **ninben** (person) 休 (rest), 体 (body), 作 (make)
旁 **tsukuri** (lit., aside)	right		斤 おのづくり **onozukuri** (ax) 近 (near), 新 (new), 所 (place)
冠 **kanmuri** (lit., crown)	top		艹 くさかんむり **kusakanmuri** (grass) 草 (grass), 花 (flower), 茶 (tea)
脚 **ashi** (lit., leg)	bottom		儿 ひとあし **hitoashi** (human legs) 見 (look), 兄 (older brother), 先 (ahead)
構 **kamae** (lit., enclosure)	frame		囗 くにがまえ **kunigamae** (border) 国 (country), 困 (be in difficulty), 囚 (prisoner)
			門 もんがまえ **mongamae** (gate) 問 (inquire), 聞 (listen), 間 (between)
			凵 うけばこ **ukebako** (container, vessel) 画 (picture), 凶 (bad), 歯 (tooth)
			匚 かくしがまえ **kakushigamae** (conceal) 区 (ward), 医 (physician), 匿 (conceal)
			勹 つつみがまえ **tsutsumigamae** (wrap) 包 (wrap), 抱 (embrace), 句 (phrase)
垂 **tare** (lit., something hanging down)	top & left		疒 やまいだれ **yamaidare** (sickness) 病 (illness), 痛 (painful), 癌 (cancer)
繞 **nyō, nyū** (lit., going around)	left & bottom		辶 しんにょう **shinnyō** (proceed) 道 (road), 進 (proceed), 過 (pass)

How do I look up a kanji in a Japanese dictionary?
Many dictionaries list kanji characters according to their pronunciation, for both on-readings and kun-readings, either in kana or in Roman letters. So, if you know the reading of a kanji character, you can easily find it in such a dictionary using its pronunciation-based index. For example, *The Original Modern Reader's Japanese-English Character Dictionary* by Andrew N. Nelson (Tuttle Publishing), has an on/kun index in the back, and kanji characters are alphabetically listed according to both their on-readings and their kun-readings in Roman letters with a unique code number provided for each character. Using that code number, you can easily find the page you should go to in the dictionary.

What if you see a kanji, but you don't know how to read it? You could then use the radical index included in most dictionaries. In a radical index, hundreds of radicals are listed according to the radical's total number of strokes. For example, 日 is the radical of 明, and it has 4 strokes. You can find the radical 日 in the radical list under the section for four-stroke radicals in just a few seconds. There you will find a code number, which will guide you to the list of all the kanji with the radical 日. For example, you will see many kanji, including 明, 晴, and 時, on the page specified by the code number for the radical 日. They are ordered according to their total stroke count. You can easily find the kanji character you want in the list.

If you have no clue about either the pronunciation or the

7

radical of the kanji, you can use the kanji's total stroke count as a reference. This book specifies the total stroke count for each kanji at the right upper corner of each page, but if you always write kanji in the correct stroke order and with the correct stroke count, you can figure it out by yourself.

How are kanji characters written?

To write kanji properly and legibly, it is very important to know how each stroke in a kanji is drawn. Here are some principles and tendencies for stroke endings, stroke directions, and stroke orders.

Stroke Endings

Each stroke ends in とめ **tome** (stop), はね **hane** (jump), or はらい **harai** (sweep). (Note that some diagonal lines end in stop-sweep.) For example, a vertical straight line can end in stop, jump, or sweep, as shown below:

とめ **tome**	はね **hane**	はらい **harai**
(stop)	(jump)	(sweep)

Stroke Directions

A stroke can be vertical, horizontal, diagonal, angled, or curved, or can be just a short abbreviated line.

Vertical lines always go from top to bottom, and *horizontal lines* always go from left to right.

Diagonal lines can go either downward or upward. For example:

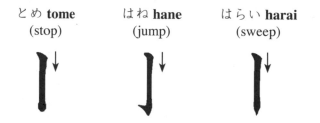

If a stroke forms a corner, a sharp angle, or a curve, it goes from left to right and then goes down, or goes down and then left to right. For example:

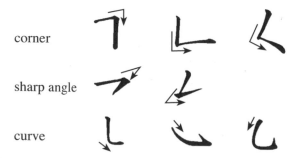

corner

sharp angle

curve

Some strokes have a combination of a sharp angle and a curve. For example:

Some strokes are extremely short and are called てん **ten**. They may be vertical or slightly diagonal:

Stroke Order

You should remember how the strokes in each character are ordered in order to write a character neatly with the appropriate shape. Most kanji characters are written following the general principles of stroke order:

1. Kanji are written from top to bottom.

   三 (three)

2. Kanji are written from left to right.

   川 (river)

3. Horizontal strokes usually precede vertical strokes when crossing, although there are some exceptions such as 王 and 田.

   十 (ten)

4. A central line usually precedes the strokes placed on its right and left.

   小 (small) 亅 小 小

5. An outer frame must be written first before finishing the inside except for the bottom line. The bottom line of an outer frame must be completed at the very end.

   国 (country) 丨 冂 国 国

6. A right-to-left diagonal stroke precedes a left-to-right diagonal stroke.

   人 (person) ノ 人

7. A vertical line piercing through the center of a character is written last.

車 (vehicle)　一　百　亘　車

8. A horizontal line piercing the center of the character is written last.

子 (child)　

How do I learn to write kanji?

Remember that a good beginning and good planning are the keys to success in learning kanji. The following are some suggested steps for learning kanji using this workbook.

Get used to the strokes

Before writing any kanji, practice drawing some of the simple strokes with different endings many times on a sheet of scrap paper. For example, try drawing the strokes presented above (e.g., vertical lines, diagonal lines). Each time you end the stroke, say とめ **tome** (stop), はね **hane** (jump), or はらい **harai** (sweep), depending on which type of ending you are working on. If you have a brush and ink, try to make changes in the thickness of different portions of each stroke. Of course, you can also use a pen or pencil. If you do, ignore the difference in the thickness of different portions of each stroke. Just get used to the general flow of strokes. It will help you to write kanji beautifully in an authentic style.

Understand the character

Before writing an actual kanji character as a whole, familiarize yourself with its meaning, pronunciation, usage examples, and radical. Be creative and make associations to help you remember the shape, composition, meaning, and sound of the character you are working on. Your associations can be logical or natural, or can be silly or funny. Your imagination and creativity will always help you learn and remember new things, especially when you are dealing with numerous items. Under each character in this book, the first several boxes show the stroke order and direction. Refer to them, and try writing the character once. The number of strokes for each kanji is specified in the upper-right corner of each page. Check whether you used the correct number of strokes when you wrote the kanji. Then compare your character with the one printed on the page. Pay attention to the size and the position of the character in relation with the box as well as the proportion and shape of the lines.

Practice writing the character

When you have fully understood the given character in terms of meaning, pronunciation, usage, radical, and stroke order, write it about 10 times in a row. You may not believe it, but your hand muscle will remember how to write a kanji if you repeat writing it many times. If helpful, trace over the gray characters at the beginning of each page.

Review kanji periodically

Practice a few new characters at a time every day following the above steps. At the end of each week, review all of the characters you learned during the week by writing them five times each. At the end of each month, review all the characters you learned during the month by writing them a few times each. If you study kanji at this pace using this workbook, you can master 100 kanji within a month or two! Sounds like a manageable plan, right? Make sure to periodically review the kanji you have learned. Flash cards can be useful, but you can also write the kanji you learned previously again and again to review them. That's why there are plenty of boxes on each page of this workbook! The point is to make an effort daily with a manageable plan for learning and reviewing kanji. Believe it or not, the more you learn, the easier it gets!

頑張ってください。
Ganbatte kudasai!
Try your best (and good luck)!

一	ON readings イチ **ICHI**, イッ **I'** KUN readings ひと- **hito-**, ひと-つ **hito-tsu**	meaning one	1 stroke radical 一

common words

一円	いちえん	**ichien**	one yen
一人	ひとり	**hitori**	one person
一日	いちにち/ついたち	**ichinichi/tsuitachi**	a day; all day/the first day (of the month)
一本	いっぽん	**ippon**	one slender object
一つ	ひとつ	**hitotsu**	one (piece; age)
一月	ひとつき	**hitotsuki**	one month
一月	いちがつ	**ichigatsu**	January
一個	いっこ	**ikko**	one (piece)

		ON readings 二 **NI** **KUN readings** ふた **futa**, ふた-つ **futa-tsu**		meaning two	2 strokes radical 二

二

common words

二月	にがつ	**Nigatsu**	February
二人	ふたり	**futari**	two people
二日	ふつか	**futsuka**	two days, 2nd day of the month
二十日	はつか	**hatsuka**	the twentieth (date); (for) twenty days
二千	にせん	**nisen**	two thousand
二百	にひゃく	**nihyaku**	two hundred
二つ	ふたつ	**futatsu**	two (pieces; age)

三	**ON readings** サン　SAN **KUN readings** み mi-, み（っ）－つ mi(t)-tsu	**meaning** three	**3 strokes** **radical** 一

common words

三角	さんかく	**sankaku**	triangle
三月	さんがつ	**Sangatsu**	March
三日	みっか	**mikka**	three days, 3rd day of the month
三時	さんじ	**sanji**	three o'clock
三十	さんじゅう	**sanjū**	thirty
三人	さんにん	**san'nin**	three people
三年	さんねん	**san'nen**	three years, the third year
三つ	み（っ）つ	**mi(t)tsu**	three (pieces; age)

	ON readings シ SHI KUN readings よ yo, よ(っ)-つ yo(t)-tsu, よん yon	meaning four	5 strokes
			radical □

四

common words

四月	しがつ	**Shigatsu**	April
四日	よっか	**yokka**	four days
四人	よにん	**yonin**	four people
四回	よんかい	**yonkai**	four times
四か月	よんかげつ	**yonkagetsu**	(for) four months
四時	よじ	**yoji**	four o'clock
四角	しかく	**shikaku**	square
四(っ)つ	よ(っ)つ	**yo(t)tsu**	four (pieces; age)

	ON readings ゴ **GO** KUN readings いつ **itsu**, いつーつ **itsu-tsu**	meaning five	4 strokes radical 二

五

common words

五日	いつか	**itsuka**	five days, 5th day of the month
五月	ごがつ	**Gogatsu**	May
五時	ごじ	**goji**	five o'clock
五千	ごせん	**gosen**	five thousand
五十	ごじゅう	**gojū**	fifty
五百	ごひゃく	**gohyaku**	five hundred
五つ	いつつ	**itsutsu**	five (pieces; age)

一　丁　丂　五　五　五　五

| | ON readings
ロク ROKU
KUN readings
む mu, む(っ)ーつ mu(t)-tsu | meaning
six | 4 strokes |
| | | | radical
八 |

六

common words

六日	むいか	**muika**	six days, 6th day of the month
六月	ろくがつ	**Rokugatsu**	June
六分	ろっぷん	**roppun**	six minutes
六時	ろくじ	**rokuji**	six o'clock
六百	ろっぴゃく	**roppyaku**	six hundred
六十	ろくじゅう	**rokujū**	sixty
六つ	む(っ)つ	**mu(t)tsu**	six (pieces; age)

七

| | ON readings
シチ SHICHI | meaning
seven | 2 strokes |
| | KUN readings
なな nana, なな－つ nana-tsu | | radical
一 |

common words

七月	しちがつ	**Shichigatsu**	July
七人	なな/しちにん	**nana/shichinin**	seven people
七日	なのか	**nanoka**	seven days, 7th day of the month
七万円	ななまんえん	**nanaman'en**	seventy thousand yen
七時	しちじ	**shichiji**	seven o'clock
七百	ななひゃく	**nanahyaku**	seven hundred
七つ	ななつ	**nanatsu**	seven (pieces; age)

一 七 七 七 七

	ON readings ハチ **HACHI** KUN readings や **ya**, や(っ)ー つ **ya(t)-tsu**	meaning eight	2 strokes
			radical 八

common words

八月	は ち が つ	**Hachigatsu**	August
八年	は ち ね ん	**hachinen**	eight years
八日	よ う か	**yōka**	eight days, 8th day of the month
八時	は ち じ	**hachiji**	eight o'clock
八十	は ち じゅ う	**hachijū**	eighty
八百	は っ ぴゃ く	**happyaku**	eight hundred
八つ	や(っ)つ	**ya(t)tsu**	eight (pieces; age)

		ON readings ク **KU**, キュウ**KYŪ** KUN readings ここの－つ **kokono-tsu**, ここの **kokono**		meaning nine	**2 strokes**
					radical 乙（乚）

common words

九月	くがつ	**Kugatsu**	September
九人	く/きゅうにん	**ku/kyūnin**	nine people
九日	ここのか	**kokonoka**	nine days, 9th day of the month
九時	くじ	**kuji**	nine o'clock
九十	きゅうじゅう	**kyūjū**	ninety
九百	きゅうひゃく	**kyūhyaku**	nine hundred
九つ	ここのつ	**kokonotsu**	nine (pieces; age)

九

ノ 九 九 九 九

	ON readings ジュウ **JŪ**, ジッ **JI'** KUN readings とお **tō**	meaning ten	2 strokes
十			radical 十

common words

十一	じゅういち	**jūichi**	eleven
十個	じゅっこ	**jukko**	ten (pieces)
十月	じゅうがつ	**Jūgatsu**	October
十日	とおか	**tōka**	ten days, 10th day of the month
十一月	じゅういちがつ	**Jūichigatsu**	November
十二	じゅうに	**jūni**	twelve
十二月	じゅうにがつ	**Jūnigatsu**	December
十分	じっぷん/じゅっぷん	**jippun/juppun**	ten minutes

	ON readings ヒャク **HYAKU** KUN readings	meaning hundred	6 strokes radical 白

百

common words

三百	さんびゃく	**sanbyaku**	three hundred
百円	ひゃくえん	**hyakuen**	one hundred yen
百人	ひゃくにん	**hyakunin**	one hundred people
何百	なんびゃく	**nanbyaku**	how many hundreds; hundreds of ~
百本	ひゃっぽん	**hyappon**	hundred (trees, bottles, or thin long things)
百枚	ひゃくまい	**hyakumai**	hundred sheets (of …)

一	丆	丆	百	百	百	百	百
百							

	ON readings セン **SEN** KUN readings ち **chi**		meaning thousand	3 strokes
千				radical 十
	common words 三千　　さんぜん　　**sanzen**　　three thousand 千円　　せんえん　　**sen'en**　　one thousand yen 千人　　せんにん　　**sen'nin**　　one thousand people 五千円　ごせんえん　**gosen'en**　five thousand yen 千代紙　ちよがみ　**chiyogami**　origami paper with colored figures 二千年　にせんねん　**nisen'nen**　two thousand years			

	ON readings マン **MAN**, バン **BAN** **KUN readings**		**meaning** ten thousand	**3 strokes**
				radical 一

万

common words

一万円	いちまんえん	**ichiman'en**	ten thousand yen
一万人	いちまんにん	**ichiman'nin**	ten thousand people
万国	ばんこく	**bankoku**	all nations
万年筆	まんねんひつ	**man'nenhitsu**	fountain pen
億万長者	おくまんちょうじゃ	**okumanchōja**	billionaire
百万円	ひゃくまんえん	**hyakuman'en**	one million yen
万人	ばんにん/ばんじん	**ban'nin/banjin**	everyone, everybody

一 万 万 万 万 万

			ON readings エン **EN** KUN readings まるーい **maru-i**		meanings circle; yen (Japa- nese monetary unit)	4 strokes
						radical 冂

円

common words

円高	えんだか	**endaka**	high value of the yen
円安	えんやす	**en'yasu**	low value of the yen
百五十円	ひゃくごじゅうえん	**hyakugojūen**	one hundred and fifty yen
円満な	えんまんな	**enman na**	harmonious
五十円	ごじゅうえん	**gojūen**	fifty yen
十円	じゅうえん	**jūen**	ten yen
円い	まるい	**marui**	circular, round

丨	冂	冂	円	円	円	円	

年

ON readings
ネン **NEN**

KUN readings
とし **toshi**

meanings
year; age

6 strokes

radical
干

common words

去年	きょねん	**kyonen**	last year
今年	ことし	**kotoshi**	this year
年金	ねんきん	**nenkin**	pension
来年	らいねん	**rainen**	next year
年れい	ねんれい	**nenrei**	age
年度	ねんど	**nendo**	fiscal/academic year
忘年会	ぼうねんかい	**bōnenkai**	year-end party

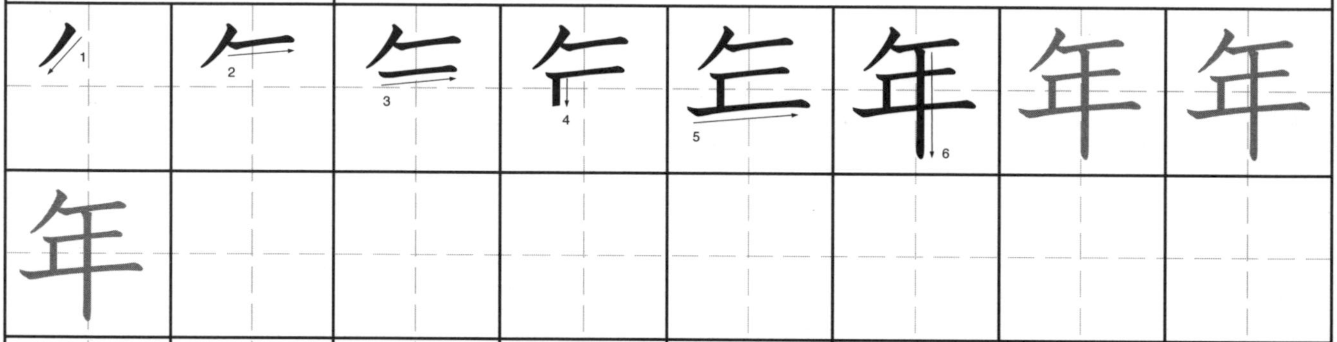

	ON readings カイ **KAI** KUN readings まわ–る **mawa-ru**, まわ–す **mawa-su**	meanings times; to turn; to go around	6 strokes
			radical □

回

common words

次回	じかい	**jikai**	the next time
回転する	かいてんする	**kaiten suru**	to rotate, to revolve
回答	かいとう	**kaitō**	answer
回る	まわる	**mawaru**	to go around
回数券	かいすうけん	**kaisūken**	coupon ticket
前回	ぜんかい	**zenkai**	the last time
二回目	にかいめ	**nikaime**	the second time

	ON readings シュウ **SHŪ** KUN readings	meaning week	11 strokes radical
週	**common words** 今週　　こんしゅう　　**konshū**　　this week 週末　　しゅうまつ　　**shūmatsu**　　weekend 先週　　せんしゅう　　**senshū**　　last week 来週　　らいしゅう　　**raishū**　　next week 週刊誌　しゅうかんし　**shūkanshi**　weekly magazine 週間　　しゅうかん　　**shūkan**　　week		

ノ¹	几²	冂³	冃⁴	用⁵	用⁶	周⁷	周⁸
周⁹	凋¹⁰	週¹¹	週	週	週		

		ON readings バン **BAN** KUN readings		meanings number; turn; to keep watch		12 strokes
						radical 田

番

common words

順番	じゅんばん	**junban**	order, one's turn
当番	とうばん	**tōban**	person on duty/watch
番組	ばんぐみ	**bangumi**	TV/radio program
番号	ばんごう	**bangō**	number
一番	いちばん	**ichiban**	number 1, the most
二番目	にばんめ	**nibanme**	the second
交番	こうばん	**kōban**	police box
番地	ばんち	**banchi**	number of a house, address

	ON readings スウ **SŪ**	meanings	**13 strokes**
	KUN readings かず **kazu**, かぞ－える **kazo-eru**	number; to count	radical 攵（攴）

数

common words

数学	すうがく	**sūgaku**	mathematics
数字	すうじ	**sūji**	figure, numeral
人数	にんずう	**ninzū**	the number of people
半数	はんすう	**hansū**	half the number
分数	ぶんすう	**bunsū**	fraction
無数(の)	むすう(の)	**musū (no)**	numerous
数える	かぞえる	**kazoeru**	to count

	ON readings ニチ **NICHI**, ジツ **JITSU** KUN readings ひ **hi**, か **ka**	meanings sun; day; counter for days	4 strokes
			radical 日

日

common words

休日	きゅうじつ	**kyūjitsu**	holiday, day off
祝日	しゅくじつ	**shukujitsu**	public holiday
たんじょう日	たんじょうび	**tanjōbi**	birthday
日本	にほん/にっぽん	**Nihon/Nippon**	Japan
今日	きょう/こんにち	**kyō/kon'nichi**	today/ nowadays
昨日	きのう/さくじつ	**kinō/sakujitsu**	yesterday
明日	あす/あした	**asu/ashita**	tomorrow

丨	冂	月	日	日	日	日	
1	2	3	4				

	ON readings ガツ **GATSU**, ゲツ **GETSU** **KUN readings** つき **tsuki**	**meanings** month; moon	**4 strokes**
			radical 月

月

common words

今月	こんげつ	**kongetsu**	this month
生年月日	せいねんがっぴ	**seinengappi**	date of birth
先月	せんげつ	**sengetsu**	last month
来月	らいげつ	**raigetsu**	next month
月給	げっきゅう	**gekkyū**	monthly salary
月見	つきみ	**tsukimi**	moon viewing party
満月	まんげつ	**mangetsu**	full moon

丿	刀	月	月	月	月	月	

	ON readings カ **KA** KUN readings ひ **hi**, ほ **ho**		meaning fire	4 strokes
				radical 火

火

common words

火山	かざん	**kazan**	volcano
火事	かじ	**kaji**	fire
花火	はなび	**hanabi**	fireworks
火花	ひばな	**hibana**	spark
火力発電	かりょくはつでん	**karyoku hatsuden**	thermal power
聖火	せいか	**seika**	sacred fire, Olympic torch
ふん火	ふんか	**funka**	explosion

丶	丷	少	火	火	火	火	
1	2	3	4				

	ON readings スイ **SUI** KUN readings みず **mizu**		meaning water	4 strokes
水	**common words** 香水　　こうすい　　**kōsui**　　　　perfume 水道　　すいどう　　**suidō**　　　　water (service) 水平な　すいへいな　**suihei na**　　horizontal 水色　　みずいろ　　**mizu iro**　　　color of the sea ふん水　ふんすい　　**funsui**　　　　fountain 水分　　すいぶん　　**suibun**　　　　moisture 冷水　　れいすい　　**reisui**　　　　ice water, cold water			radical 水

	ON readings モク **MOKU** KUN readings き **ki**		meanings tree, wood	**4 strokes** radical 木

木

common words

つみ木	つみき	**tsumiki**	building blocks
木材	もくざい	**mokuzai**	lumber, wood
木製	もくせい	**mokusei**	made of wood, wooden
植木	うえき	**ueki**	garden tree/plant
木かげ	こかげ	**kokage**	the shade of the tree
大木	たいぼく	**taiboku**	large stout tree
木造	もくぞう	**mokuzō**	wooden, made of wood

一 十 オ 木 木 木 木

	ON readings キン **KIN**, コン **KON** **KUN readings** かな **kana**, かね **kane**		**meanings** gold, metal; money	**8 strokes**
金	**common words**			**radical** 金

common words

お金	おかね	**okane**	money
金づち	かなづち	**kanazuchi**	hammer; a person who cannot swim
現金	げんきん	**genkin**	cash
金あみ	かなあみ	**kana-ami**	woven wire
税金	ぜいきん	**zeikin**	tax, duty
針金	はりがね	**harigane**	wire
金メダル	きんメダル	**kinmedaru**	gold medal

ノ	人	今	今	全	全	金	金
金	金	金					

		ON readings ド **DO**, ト **TO** KUN readings つち **tsuchi**		meanings earth, soil	3 strokes
					radical 土

common words

国土	こくど	**kokudo**	(national) country
土台	どだい	**dodai**	base, foundation
土産	みやげ	**miyage**	souvenir, gift
土木工事	どぼくこうじ	**dobokukōji**	public works
赤土	あかつち	**akatsuchi**	reddish soil
土地	とち	**tochi**	ground, plot of land
土木	どぼく	**doboku**	civil engineering

一 十 土 土 土 土

	ON readings ヨウ **YŌ** KUN readings		meaning days of the week	18 strokes radical 日

曜

common words

何曜日	なんようび	**nan'yōbi**	what day of the week
月曜日	げつようび	**Getsuyōbi**	Monday
火曜日	かようび	**Kayōbi**	Tuesday
水曜日	すいようび	**Suiyōbi**	Wednesday
木曜日	もくようび	**Mokuyōbi**	Thursday
金曜日	きんようび	**Kin'yōbi**	Friday
土曜日	どようび	**Doyōbi**	Saturday
日曜日	にちようび	**Nichiyōbi**	Sunday

	ON readings ゴ GO KUN readings	meaning noon	4 strokes
午			radical 十

common words

午後	ごご	**gogo**	afternoon, P.M.
午前	ごぜん	**gozen**	morning, A.M.
午前れい時	ごぜんれいじ	**gozenreiji**	midnight
正午	しょうご	**shōgo**	noon
午後二時	ごごにじ	**gogoniji**	two o'clock, two P. M.

ノ 仁 仁 午 午 午 午

今

	ON readings コン **KON**, キン **KIN** KUN readings いま **ima**		meanings now, the present	4 strokes
				radical 人

common words

今すぐ	いますぐ	**imasugu**	right now
今回	こんかい	**konkai**	this time
今度	こんど	**kondo**	next time
今晩	こんばん	**konban**	tonight
今春	こんしゅん	**konshun**	this spring
ただ今	ただいま	**tadaima**	right now; I'm home!
今後	こんご	**kongo**	future, from now

ノ¹	人²	今³	今⁴	今	今	今	

分	**ON readings** ブン **BUN**, フン **FUN** **KUN readings** わーける **wa-keru**, わーかる **wa-karu**	**meanings** to divide, portion; minute	**4 strokes** **radical** 刀

common words

三日分	みっかぶん	**mikkabun**	three days' worth
四分	よんぷん	**yonpun**	four minutes
自分	じぶん	**jibun**	self
成分	せいぶん	**seibun**	ingredient, component
部分	ぶぶん	**bubun**	part(s), portion, section
分かる	わかる	**wakaru**	to understand
分ける	わける	**wakeru**	to divide

ノ	八	分	分	分	分	分	

半

ON readings
ハン **HAN**

KUN readings
なか-ば **naka-ba**

meaning
half

5 strokes

radical
十

common words

一時半	いちじはん	**ichijihan**	half past one
半年	はんとし	**hantoshi**	half a year
半日	はんにち	**han'nichi**	half a day
半分	はんぶん	**hanbun**	half
半がく	はんがく	**hangaku**	half price, Half Off!
前半	ぜんはん／ぜんぱん	**zenhan/zenpan**	the first half
半ば	なかば	**nakaba**	middle, halfway

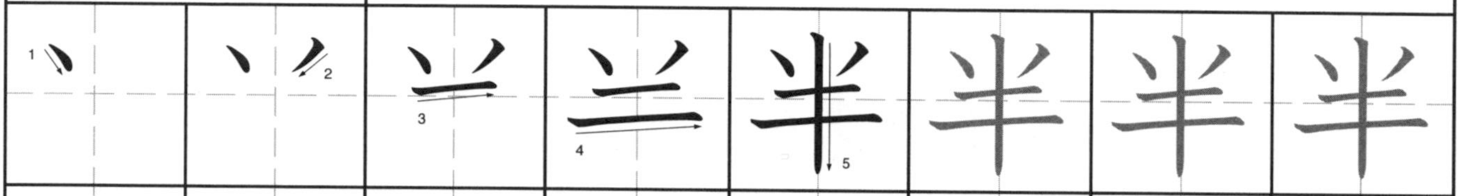

	ON readings マイ MAI KUN readings	meanings every, each	6 strokes
			radical 毋

毎

common words

毎週	まいしゅう	**maishū**	every week
毎月	まいつき	**maitsuki**	every month
毎日	まいにち	**mainichi**	every day
毎回	まいかい	**maikai**	every time
毎食	まいしょく	**maishoku**	each/every meal
毎晩	まいばん	**maiban**	every night
毎年	まいとし/まいねん	**maitoshi/mainen**	every year

	ON readings チョウ **CHŌ** KUN readings あさ **asa**	meaning morning	12 strokes
朝			radical 月

common words

朝市	あさいち	**asaichi**	morning market
朝ごはん	あさごはん	**asagohan**	breakfast
朝食	ちょうしょく	**chōshoku**	breakfast
朝刊	ちょうかん	**chōkan**	morning paper
今朝	けさ	**kesa**	this morning
朝日	あさひ	**asahi**	morning sun
毎朝	まいあさ	**maiasa**	every morning

一¹	十²	亠³	古⁴	古⁵	直⁶	卓⁷	卓⁸
軪⁹	朝¹⁰	朝¹¹	朝	朝¹²	朝	朝

	ON readings チュウ **CHŪ** KUN readings ひる **hiru**	meanings daytime; noon	9 strokes radical 日

昼

common words

昼食	ちゅうしょく	**chūshoku**	lunch
昼ごはん	ひるごはん	**hirugohan**	lunch
昼間	ひるま	**hiruma**	daytime
昼休み	ひるやすみ	**hiruyasumi**	lunchtime
真昼	まひる	**mahiru**	midday, noon
昼寝	ひるね	**hirune**	nap

㇈	⼎	尸	尺	尺	昦	昬	昼
昼	昼	昼	昼				

	ON readings ヤ **YA** KUN readings よ **yo**, よる **yoru**		meanings evening, night	8 strokes radical 夕

夜

common words

今夜	こんや	**kon'ya**	tonight
夜間	やかん	**yakan**	nighttime
夜食	やしょく	**yashoku**	late-night snack
夜中	よなか	**yonaka**	midnight
深夜	しんや	**shin'ya**	late-evening
昨夜	さくや	**sakuya**	last night
夜明け	よあけ	**yoake**	dawn

	ON readings カ **KA** KUN readings なに **nani**, なん **nan**	meanings what, how many	7 strokes radical 亻

何

common words

何回	なんかい	**nankai**	how many times
何月	なんがつ	**nangatsu**	what month
何年	なんねん	**nan'nen**	what year
何日	なんにち	**nan'nichi**	what day
何時	なんじ	**nanji**	what time
何時間	なんじかん	**nanjikan**	how many hours
何人	なんにん	**nan'nin**	how many people
何分	なんぷん	**nanpun**	how many minutes

ノ	亻	仁	仃	何	何	何	何
何	何						

	ON readings ジ JI KUN readings とき toki		meanings hour; time	10 strokes
				radical 日

時

common words

一時間	いちじかん	**ichijikan**	one hour
時間	じかん	**jikan**	time, hour
時代	じだい	**jidai**	period (of time), era, age
時々	ときどき	**tokidoki**	sometimes
当時	とうじ	**tōji**	at that time
同時に	どうじに	**dōji ni**	at the same time
日時	にちじ	**nichiji**	the date and time

丨	冂	日	日	日	日	旪	旹
時	時	時	時	時			

	ON readings ケイ **KEI** **KUN readings** はかーる **haka-ru**, はかーらう **haka-rau**	meanings to measure; to plan; to arrange	9 strokes radical 言

計

common words

会計	かいけい	**kaikei**	accounts, bill; cashier
計画する	けいかくする	**keikaku suru**	to plan
計算する	けいさんする	**keisan suru**	to calculate
時計	とけい	**tokei**	watch, clock
温度計	おんどけい	**ondokei**	thermometer
合計する	ごうけいする	**gōkei suru**	to total, to add up
小計	しょうけい	**shōkei**	subtotal
計る	はかる	**hakaru**	to measure

	ON readings カン **KAN**, ケン **KEN** KUN readings あいだ **aida**, ま **ma**	meanings between; space, interval	12 strokes
			radical 門

間

common words

仲間	なかま	**nakama**	partner, friend
年間(の)	ねんかん(の)	**nenkan no**	annual
何週間	なんしゅうかん	**nanshūkan**	how many weeks
何日間	なんにちかん	**nan'nichikan**	how many days
居間	いま	**ima**	living room
この間	このあいだ	**konoaida**	the other day
人間	にんげん	**ningen**	human being
三日間	みっかかん	**mikkakan**	(for) three days

｜	冂	冂	冃	冃	門	門	門
1	2	3	4	5	6	7	8

門	間	間	間	間	間	間	
9	10	11	12				

ON readings	meanings	7 strokes
ダン **DAN**, ナン **NAN**	man, male	
KUN readings		**radical**
おとこ **otoko**		田

男

common words

男の子	おとこのこ	**otokonoko**	boy
次男	じなん	**jinan**	second son
男子	だんし	**danshi**	man, boy
男らしい	おとこらしい	**otokorashii**	masculine
男女	だんじょ	**danjo**	men and women
男性	だんせい	**dansei**	male
長男	ちょうなん	**chōnan**	eldest son

	ON readings ジョ **JO**, ニョ **NYO**, ニョウ **NYŌ** KUN readings おんな **on'na**, め **me**	meanings woman, female	3 strokes
			radical 女

女

common words

少女	しょうじょ	**shōjo**	girl, maiden
女王	じょおう	**jo'ō**	queen
女性	じょせい	**josei**	female
女房	にょうぼう	**nyōbō**	wife
女子	じょし	**joshi**	woman, girl
女子大	じょしだい	**joshidai**	women's university/college
女の子	おんなのこ	**on'nanoko**	girl

く 女 女 女 女 女

	ON readings フ **FU** KUN readings ちち **chichi**		meaning father	4 strokes
				radical 父

父

common words

お父さん	おとうさん	**otōsan**	father
祖父	そふ	**sofu**	grandfather
父親	ちちおや	**chichioya**	father, male parent
父母	ふぼ	**fubo**	father and mother, parents
神父	しんぷ	**shinpu**	(Christian) priest, father
義父	ぎふ	**gifu**	father-in-law
父上	ちちうえ	**chichiue**	father (polite)

ノ　ハ　少　父　父　父　父

		ON readings		meaning		5 strokes
		ボ **BO**		mother		
		KUN readings				**radical**
		はは haha				母

母

common words

お母さん	おかあさん	**okāsan**	mother
祖母	そぼ	**sobo**	grandmother
母親	ははおや	**hahaoya**	mother, female parent
母国	ぼこく	**bokoku**	mother country
母音	ぼいん/ぼおん	**boin/bo'on**	vowel (sound)
母国語	ぼこくご	**bokokugo**	first language, mother tongue
母上	ははうえ	**hahaue**	mother (polite)

	ON readings シン SHIN	meanings parent; familiar	16 strokes
	KUN readings おや oya, した-しい shita-shii, した-しむ shita-shimu		radical 見

親

common words

親指	おやゆび	**oyayubi**	thumb
親切な	しんせつな	**shinsetsu na**	kindly, friendly
両親	りょうしん	**ryōshin**	parents
親日	しんにち	**shin'nichi**	pro-Japanese
親類	しんるい	**shinrui**	relative
親子	おやこ	**oyako**	parent and child
親しい	したしい	**shitashii**	familiar
親しむ	したしむ	**shitashimu**	get familiar with

ON readings シ SHI, ス SU KUN readings こ ko		meaning child	3 strokes
			radical 子

子

common words

菓子	かし	**kashi**	candy, snack, sweet
原子	げんし	**genshi**	atom
帽子	ぼうし	**bōshi**	hat
息子	むすこ	**musuko**	son
利子	りし	**rishi**	interest
子ども(たち)	こども(たち)	**kodomo(tachi)**	child(ren)

了 了 子 子 子 子

	ON readings ケイ **KEI**, キョウ **KYŌ** KUN readings あに **ani**		meaning elder brother	5 strokes

兄

common words

兄貴	あにき	**aniki**	elder brother (familiar)
義兄	ぎけい	**gikei**	brother-in-law
実兄	じっけい	**jikkei**	real elder brother
お兄さん	おにいさん	**oniisan**	elder brother (polite), young male
兄弟	きょうだい	**kyōdai**	brothers
父兄	ふけい	**fukei**	guardians

radical

儿

⎮	口	口	尸	兄	兄	兄	兄

	ON readings テイ **TEI**, ダイ **DAI** KUN readings おとうと **otōto**		meaning younger brother	7 strokes
				radical 弓

弟

common words

義弟	ぎてい	**gitei**	brother-in-law
弟さん	おとうとさん	**otōtosan**	(your) younger brother (polite)
門弟	もんてい	**montei**	follower
子弟	してい	**shitei**	sons, children
弟妹	ていまい	**teimai**	younger brothers and sisters
弟子	でし	**deshi**	pupil, disciple

ヽ 1	ヽソ 2	沙 3	当 4	肖 5	弟 6	弟 7	弟
弟	弟						

	ON readings シ **SHI** KUN readings あね **ane**	meaning elder sister	8 strokes
			radical 女

姉

common words

実姉	じっし	**jisshi**	real elder sister
姉上	あねうえ	**ane'ue**	elder sister (polite)
義姉	ぎし	**gishi**	sister-in-law
長姉	ちょうし	**chōshi**	eldest sister
姉弟	してい	**shitei**	sister and brother
お姉さん	おねえさん	**onēsan**	elder sister (polite), young lady

く	女	女	女	女	姉	姉	姉
姉	姉	姉					

ON readings マイ **MAI** **KUN readings** いもうと **imōto**	**meaning** younger sister	**8 strokes** **radical** 女

妹

common words

姉妹　　　しまい　　　　**shimai**　　　　sisters
義妹　　　ぎまい　　　　**gimai**　　　　sister-in-law
妹さん　　いもうとさん　**imōtosan**　　(your) younger sister (polite)

く	タ	女	女一	女二	圤	妹	妹
妹	妹	妹					

	ON readings シ **SHI** **KUN readings** わたくし **watakushi**, わたし **watashi**	**meanings** private; I	**7 strokes** **radical** 禾

私

common words

私生活	しせいかつ	**shiseikatsu**	private life
私物	しぶつ	**shibutsu**	private property
私用	しよう	**shiyō**	private engagement
私立	しりつ	**shiritsu**	private (institution)
私書箱	ししょばこ	**shishobako**	P.O. Box
私鉄	してつ	**shitetsu**	private railway
私服	しふく	**shifuku**	plain/private clothes

一	二	千	禾	禾	私	私	私
私	私						

	ON readings ユウ YŪ	meaning	4 strokes
		friend	radical
	KUN readings とも tomo		又

友

common words

級友	きゅうゆう	**kyūyū**	classmate
戦友	せんゆう	**sen'yū**	comrades in arms
友好	ゆうこう	**yūkō**	friendship
親友	しんゆう	**shin'yū**	close friend
友だち	ともだち	**tomodachi**	friend
友情	ゆうじょう	**yūjō**	friendship
友人	ゆうじん	**yūjin**	friend

一 ナ 方 友 友 友 友

ON readings コウ **KŌ**, ク **KU**	meaning	3 strokes
KUN readings く ち **kuchi**, ぐ ち **guchi**	mouth	radical 口

口

common words

入口	いりぐち	**iriguchi**	entrance
口笛	くちぶえ	**kuchibue**	whistle
人口	じんこう	**jinkō**	population
出口	でぐち	**deguchi**	exit
改札口	かいさつぐち	**kaisatsuguchi**	ticket gate, wicket
口座	こうざ	**kōza**	bank account
窓口	まどぐち	**madoguchi**	window (in a public office, bank, or station)
中央口	ちゅうおうぐち	**chūōguchi**	central exit

		ON readings シュ SHU KUN readings て te		meaning hand	4 strokes

radical
手

手

common words			
手数料	てすうりょう	**tesūryō**	fee, charge, commission
助手	じょしゅ	**joshu**	research associate, assistant
選手	せんしゅ	**senshu**	athlete
握手	あくしゅ	**akushu**	handshake
歌手	かしゅ	**kashu**	singer
手紙	てがみ	**tegami**	letter
手袋	てぶくろ	**tebukuro**	gloves

		ON readings シン SHIN KUN readings こころ kokoro		meanings spirit, heart, mind	4 strokes
					radical 心

心

common words

安心	あんしん	**anshin**	ease of mind
心ぞう	しんぞう	**shinzō**	heart
心配	しんぱい	**shinpai**	worry, anxiety
中心	ちゅうしん	**chūshin**	center, core; focus
関心	かんしん	**kanshin**	interest, concern
初心者	しょしんしゃ	**shoshinsha**	beginner
身心	しんしん	**shinshin**	body and mind
野心	やしん	**yashin**	ambition

ON readings モク **MOKU**, ボク **BOKU** **KUN readings** め **me**, ま **ma**	**meaning** eye	**5 strokes**	
		radical 目	

目

common words

一日目	いちにちめ	**ichinichime**	the first day
科目	かもく	**kamoku**	course subject
目下	めした	**meshita**	one's subordinate
目上	めうえ	**meue**	one's superior
種目	しゅもく	**shumoku**	item
目印	めじるし	**mejirushi**	mark
目次	もくじ	**mokuji**	table of contents
目的	もくてき	**mokuteki**	purpose

	ON readings ソク SOKU KUN readings あし ashi, たーりる ta-riru, たーす ta-su		meanings foot, leg	7 strokes
足	**common words** 不足　　ふそく　　　**fusoku**　　　insufficiency 満足　　まんぞく　　**manzoku**　　satisfaction 一足　　いっそく　　**issoku**　　　a pair of (shoes or footwear) 遠足　　えんそく　　**ensoku**　　　excursion 足下　　あしもと　　**ashimoto**　　at one's feet 土足　　どそく　　　**dosoku**　　　with shoes on 足す　　たす　　　　**tasu**　　　　to add 足りる　たりる　　　**tariru**　　　to be enough			radical 足

ヽ₁	口₂	口₃	卫₄	卫₅	足₆	足₇	足
足	足						

		meaning	7 strokes
	ON readings タイ **TAI**, テイ **TEI** **KUN readings** からだ **karada**	body	
体			**radical** 亻

common words

体育	たいいく	**tai'iku**	physical education
体力	たいりょく	**tairyoku**	physical strength
団体	だんたい	**dantai**	a group
体育館	たいいくかん	**tai'ikukan**	gymnasium
体温計	たいおんけい	**taionkei**	clinical thermometer
体験	たいけん	**taiken**	experience
体重	たいじゅう	**taijū**	(body) weight
体制	たいせい	**taisei**	system

ノ	イ	什	什	体	体	体	体
体	体						

	ON readings トウ **TŌ,** ズ **ZU,** ト **TO** **KUN readings** あたま **atama,** かしら **kashira**	**meanings** head, top, leader, brain	**16 strokes** **radical** 頁

頭

common words

頭文字	かしらもじ	**kashira moji**	initial character
頭取	とうどり	**tōdori**	president (commonly bank or company)
頭上注意	ずじょうちゅうい	**zujōchūi**	watch your head
教頭	きょうとう	**kyōtō**	head teacher
頭痛	ずつう	**zutsū**	headache
頭脳	ずのう	**zunō**	brain, head
先頭	せんとう	**sentō**	top, leader, head

	ON readings ガン GAN		meaning face		18 strokes
	KUN readings かお kao				radical 頁

顔

common words

顔色	かおいろ	**kaoiro**	complexion
顔付	かおつき	**kaotsuki**	face, look, countenance
顔面	がんめん	**ganmen**	face
童顔	どうがん	**dōgan**	baby face
横顔	よこがお	**yokogao**	profile
丸顔	まるがお	**marugao**	round face
顔立ち	かおだち	**kaodachi**	countenance
新顔	しんがお	**shingao**	newcomer

丶 1	亠 2	六 3	立 4	立 5	产 6	产 7	彦 8
彦 9	彦 10	彦 11	颜 12	颜 13	顔 14	顔 15	顔 16
顔 17	顔 18	顔	顔	顔			

	ON readings ジ **JI** KUN readings みみ **mimi**	meaning ear	6 strokes
			radical 耳

耳

common words

早耳	はやみみ	**hayamimi**	keen of hearing
耳打ち	みみうち	**mimiuchi**	whispering
耳が遠い	みみがとおい	**mimi ga tōi**	hard of hearing
耳鳴り	みみなり	**miminari**	ringing in the ears
耳あて	みみあて	**mimiate**	earmuffs
耳かき	みみかき	**mimikaki**	earpick
耳飾り	みみかざり	**mimikazari**	earring
耳たぶ	みみたぶ	**mimitabu**	ear lobe

左	ON readings サ SA KUN readings ひだり hidari	meaning left	5 strokes radical 工

common words

左派	さは	saha	leftist (political), left wing
左側	ひだりがわ	hidarigawa	left side
左利き(の)	ひだりきき(の)	hidarikiki (no)	southpaw
左手	ひだりて	hidarite	left hand
左右	さゆう	sayū	left and right
左折禁止	させつきんし	sasetsu kinshi	No Left Turn

一　ナ　ナ　左　左　左　左　左

	ON readings ウ **U**, ユウ **YŪ** KUN readings みぎ **migi**	meaning right	5 strokes
			radical 口

右

common words

右折する	うせつする	**usetsu suru**	to make a right turn
右側	みぎがわ	**migigawa**	right side
右手	みぎて	**migite**	right hand
右往左往	うおうさおう	**uōsaō**	helter-skelter
右腕	みぎうで	**migiude**	right arm, right-hand person
右折禁止	うせつきんし	**usetsu kinshi**	No Right Turn

一 ナ 大 右 右 右 右 右

	ON readings ゼン ZEN KUN readings まえ mae		meanings before, in front of, previous	9 strokes radical リ

前

common words

以前	いぜん	**izen**	since, ago, before
前後	ぜんご	**zengo**	before and after, context
～年(日)前	～ねん(にち)まえ	**... nen(nichi)mae**	... years (days) ago
前金	まえきん	**maekin**	advance (money)
事前に	じぜんに	**jizen ni**	in advance
前日	ぜんじつ	**zenjitsu**	the previous day

	ON readings ゴ GO, コウ KŌ KUN readings うし－ろ ushi-ro, のち nochi, あと ato	meanings behind; after; the remainder	9 strokes
			radical 彳

後

common words

後半	こうはん	**kōhan**	last half, second half
最後	さいご	**saigo**	last
食後	しょくご	**shokugo**	after a meal
〜年(日)後	〜ねん(にち)ご	**... nen(nichi)go**	… years (days) after
以後	いご	**igo**	afterward
後方	こうほう	**kōhō**	rear
後日	ごじつ	**gojitsu**	at a later date, future

彳 (1) 彳 (2) 彳 (3) 彳 (4) 彳 (5) 彳 (6) 後 (7) 後 (8)

後 (9) 後 後 後

	ON readings ジョウ **JŌ**, ショウ **SHŌ** **KUN readings** うえ **ue**, あ－げる **a-geru**, あ－がる **a-garu**, の－ぼる **no-boru**, うわ **uwa**, かみ **kami**	**meanings** top, above, on; upper	**3 strokes** **radical** 一

上

common words

屋上	おくじょう	**okujō**	housetop, roof
上り	のぼり	**nobori**	up, ascent
上級	じょうきゅう	**jōkyū**	advanced course
年上の	としうえの	**toshiue no**	elder
上がる	あがる	**agaru**	to rise
上げる	あげる	**ageru**	to raise
上ぼる	のぼる	**noboru**	to go up
上流	じょうりゅう	**jōryū**	upper class; upstream

		ON readings チュウ **CHŪ** KUN readings なか **naka**		meanings middle; within; inside	4 strokes
					radical |

中

common words

一日中	いちにちじゅう	**ichinichijū**	all day long
使用中	しようちゅう	**shiyōchū**	in use, occupied
中古	ちゅうこ	**chūko**	used, secondhand
日本中	にほんじゅう	**Nihonjū**	throughout Japan
集中	しゅうちゅう	**shūchū**	concentration
中央	ちゅうおう	**chūō**	center, central; middle, midst
中学校	ちゅうがっこう	**chūgakkō**	Junior High School
中級	ちゅうきゅう	**chūkyū**	intermediate grade

\|¹ 口² 口³ 中⁴ 中 中 中

	ON readings ゲ **GE**, カ **KA** KUN readings した **shita**, しも **shimo**, もと **moto**, さ-げる **sa-geru**, さ-がる **sa-garu**, く だ-る **kuda-ru**, く だ-す **kuda-su**, く だ-さる **kuda-saru**, お-りる **o-riru**	meanings bottom, under; base; lower	3 strokes
下			radical 一

common words

下り	くだり	**kudari**	down, descent
下着	したぎ	**shitagi**	underwear
下町	したまち	**shitamachi**	downtown
地下	ちか	**chika**	underground
下りる	おりる	**oriru**	to descend; to go down
下さる	くださる	**kudasaru**	to give, to bestow
下る	くだる	**kudaru**	to go down
下げる	さげる	**sageru**	to hang
下がる	さがる	**sagaru**	to hang down
下す	くだす	**kudasu**	let down; to confer

	ON readings ナイ NAI, ダイ DAI KUN readings うち uchi	meanings inside; home; within	4 strokes
			radical 冂

内

common words

案内	あんない	**annai**	guidance, invitation
内側	うちがわ	**uchigawa**	inside
国内	こくない	**kokunai**	domestic, internal
内容	ないよう	**naiyō**	contents
家内	かない	**kanai**	my wife
市内	しない	**shinai**	inside a city, civic
都内	とない	**tonai**	inside Tokyo
内科	ないか	**naika**	internal medicine unit; internal medicine

丨	冂	内	内	内	内	内	

	ON readings ガイ **GAI**, ゲ **GE** KUN readings そと **soto**, ほか **hoka**	meanings outside; foreign; other	5 strokes
外			radical 夕

common words

外交	がいこう	**gaikō**	diplomacy
外出する	がいしゅつする	**gaishutsu suru**	to go out
外来	がいらい	**gairai**	coming from outside
時間外	じかんがい	**jikangai**	overtime
外国(人)	がいこく(じん)	**gaikoku(jin)**	foreign country (people)
外科	げか	**geka**	surgery
外側	そとがわ	**sotogawa**	outside
野外	やがい	**yagai**	outdoors

ノ　クタ　タ　外　外　外　外　外

	ON readings ホク **HOKU** KUN readings きた **kita**	meaning north	5 strokes
北			radical 匕

common words

敗北	はいぼく	**haiboku**	defeat
東北地方	とうほくちほう	**Tōhoku chihō**	Tohoku district
北部	ほくぶ	**hokubu**	northern district/part
北風	きたかぜ	**kitakaze**	north wind
北口	きたぐち	**kitaguchi**	north exit/gate
北国	きたぐに	**kitaguni**	northland
北極	ほっきょく	**Hokkyoku**	North Pole

一　才　丰　扌　北　北　北　北

ON readings セイ SEI, サイ SAI	meaning west	6 strokes
KUN readings にし nishi		radical 西

common words

西部	せいぶ	**seibu**	western district/part
関西	かんさい	**Kansai**	Kansai area
東西	とうざい	**tōzai**	east and west
西洋	せいよう	**seiyō**	the West, the Occident
西暦	せいれき	**seireki**	the dominical year (A.D.)
大西洋	たいせいよう	**Taiseiyō**	Atlantic Ocean
西口	にしぐち	**nishiguchi**	west exit/gate

西

	ON readings トウ **TŌ**	meaning east	**8 strokes**
	KUN readings ひがし **higashi**		radical 木

東

common words

中東	ちゅうとう	**Chūtō**	Middle East
関東	かんとう	**Kantō**	Kanto (district)
東西南北	とうざいなんぼく	**tōzainanboku**	east, west, south and north
東京	とうきょう	**Tōkyō**	Tokyo
東洋	とうよう	**Tōyō**	the East, the Orient
東側	ひがしがわ	**higashigawa**	east side
東口	ひがしぐち	**higashiguchi**	east exit/gate

一 厂 冂 㐄 百 車 東 東

東 東 東

	ON readings ナン NAN KUN readings みなみ minami	meaning south	9 strokes
南			radical 十

common words

南極	なんきょく	**Nankyoku**	South Pole
南米	なんべい	**Nanbei**	South America
南風	みなみかぜ	**minamikaze**	south wind
南口	みなみぐち	**minamiguchi**	south exit/gate
東南アジア	とうなんアジア	**Tōnan Ajia**	Southeast Asia
南アメリカ	みなみアメリカ	**Minami Amerika**	South America
南国	なんごく	**nangoku**	southern provinces/ country

一	十	广	币	两	南	南	南
南	南	南	南				

	ON readings	meaning	5 strokes
	ハク **HAKU**, ビャク **BYAKU**	white	radical
	KUN readings		
	しろ **shiro**, しろーい **shiro-i**		白

白

common words

面白い	おもしろい	**omoshiroi**	interesting
空白	くうはく	**kūhaku**	blank
白人	はくじん	**hakujin**	Caucasian (people)
白鳥	はくちょう	**hakuchō**	swan
純白	じゅんぱく	**junpaku**	whiteness
白衣	はくい	**hakui**	white coat
白紙	はくし	**hakushi**	blank paper
白い	しろい	**shiroi**	white

	ON readings セキ **SEKI**, シャク **SHAKU** KUN readings あか **aka**, あか‐い **aka-i**, あか‐らめ る **aka-rameru**, あか‐らむ **aka-ramu**	meaning red	7 strokes
			radical 赤

赤

common words

赤ちゃん	あかちゃん	**akachan**	baby
赤十字	せきじゅうじ	**sekijūji**	Red Cross
赤道	せきどう	**sekidō**	equator
真っ赤な	まっかな	**makka na**	bright/clear red, crimson
赤字	あかじ	**akaji**	deficit, (in the) red
赤面	せきめん	**sekimen**	blush
赤い	あかい	**akai**	red

一 十 圡 寺 赤 赤 赤 赤

赤 赤

ON readings セイ SEI, ショウ SHŌ KUN readings あお ao, あおーい ao-i	meanings blue; green; pale; inexperienced	8 strokes
		radical 青

青

common words

青白い	あおじろい	**aojiroi**	pale
青空	あおぞら	**aozora**	blue sky
青年	せいねん	**seinen**	youth
真っ青	まっさお	**massao**	paleness
青葉	あおば	**aoba**	green leaf, greenery
青少年	せいしょうねん	**seishōnen**	youth
青信号	あおしんごう	**aoshingō**	green (traffic) light
青い	あおい	**aoi**	blue; green; inexperienced

一 十 丰 圭 青 青 青 青

青 青 青

	ON readings チャ CHA, サ SA KUN readings		meanings tea (plant); brown	9 strokes
				radical 艹

茶

common words

紅茶	こうちゃ	**kōcha**	(black) tea
茶道	さどう/ちゃどう	**sadō/chadō**	tea ceremony
茶色	ちゃいろ	**chairo**	brown (color)
茶わん	ちゃわん	**chawan**	teacup, rice bowl
ウーロン茶	ウーロンちゃ	**ūroncha**	oolong tea
きっ茶店	きっさてん	**kissaten**	café
無茶な	むちゃな	**mucha na**	impossible
緑茶	りょくちゃ	**ryokucha**	green tea

一 艹 艹 サ 艾 苓 苓 茶

茶 茶 茶 茶

ON readings コク **KOKU**	meaning black	11 strokes
KUN readings くろ **kuro**, くろ-い **kuro-i**		radical 黒

黒

common words

暗黒	あんこく	**ankoku**	darkness, blackness
黒板	こくばん	**kokuban**	blackboard
白黒	しろくろ	**shirokuro**	black-and-white
真っ黒な	まっくろな	**makkuro na**	inky-black, jet-black
黒海	こっかい	**kokkai**	the Black Sea
黒字	くろじ	**kuroji**	(in the) black
黒い	くろい	**kuroi**	black

	ON readings ショク SHOKU, シキ SHIKI	meaning	6 strokes
	KUN readings いろ iro	color	radical 色

色

common words

景色	けしき	**keshiki**	scenery
色彩	しきさい	**shikisai**	color, hue
金色	きんいろ	**kin'iro**	gold, golden color
色えんぴつ	いろえんぴつ	**iroenpitsu**	colored pencil
色紙	しきし	**shikishi**	square piece of fancy paper
特色	とくしょく	**tokushoku**	characteristic
難色	なんしょく	**nanshoku**	disapproval
色々な	いろいろな	**iroiro na**	various

ノ	ク	夕	各	色	色	色	色
色							

	ON readings セン SEN	meanings	3 strokes
		river, stream	radical
川	KUN readings かわ kawa		川

common words

河川	かせん	**kasen**	river, stream
川辺	かわべ	**kawabe**	riverside
川岸	かわぎし	**kawagishi**	riverbank
川上	かわかみ	**kawakami**	upriver
小川	おがわ	**ogawa**	stream
川下	かわしも	**kawashimo**	downstream

ノ	川	川	川	川	川		

山	**ON readings** サン **SAN** **KUN readings** やま **yama**	**meaning** mountain
		3 strokes
		radical 山

common words

富士山	ふじさん	**Fujisan**	Mt. Fuji
山火事	やまかじ	**yamakaji**	wildfire
山のぼり	やまのぼり	**yamanobori**	mountain climbing
山盛り(の)	やまもり(の)	**yamamori (no)**	heap(ing)
氷山	ひょうざん	**hyōzan**	iceberg
山道	やまみち	**yamamichi**	mountain road
山手線	やまのてせん	**Yamanote-sen**	Yamanote line

	ON readings ヤ **YA** KUN readings の **no**		meanings field, plain	11 strokes radical 里

野

common words

野球	やきゅう	**yakyū**	baseball
野外	やがい	**yagai**	outdoors
野生(の)	やせいの	**yasei (no)**	wild, natural
野原	のはら	**nohara**	field
分野	ぶんや	**bun'ya**	field (of endeavor)
平野	へいや	**heiya**	a plain
野菜	やさい	**yasai**	vegetable
野山	のやま	**noyama**	hills and fields

丨₁	冂₂	冃₃	曰₄	甲₅	甶₆	里₇	里₈
野₉	野₁₀	野₁₁	野	野	野		

ON readings		meaning	5 strokes
デン **DEN**		rice field	
KUN readings			**radical**
た **ta**			田

田

common words

田園	でんえん	**den'en**	rural districts, fields and gardens
田んぼ	たんぼ	**tanbo**	rice field
田植え	たうえ	**taue**	rice planting
田舎	いなか	**inaka**	countryside
油田	ゆでん	**yuden**	oilfield

	ON readings セキ **SEKI**, シャク **SHAKU**, コク **KOKU** **KUN readings** いし **ishi**	meaning stone	**5 strokes** **radical** 石

石

	common words			
	小石	こいし	**koishi**	pebble
	石炭	せきたん	**sekitan**	coal
	磁石	じしゃく	**jishaku**	magnet
	宝石	ほうせき	**hōseki**	gem, jewel
	石けん	せっけん	**sekken**	soap
	石橋	いしばし	**ishibashi**	stone bridge
	石庭	せきてい	**sekitei**	stone garden
	石油	せきゆ	**sekiyu**	oil

一 丆 不 石 石 石 石 石

	ON readings カ **KA** KUN readings はな **hana**	meaning flower	7 strokes radical 艹

花

common words

花びん	かびん	**kabin**	vase
花屋	はなや	**hanaya**	flower shop, florist
生け花	いけばな	**ikebana**	(Japanese) flower arrangement
花たば	はなたば	**hanataba**	bouquet
お花見	おはなみ	**o-hanami**	cherry blossom viewing
花よめ	はなよめ	**hanayome**	bride
国花	こっか	**kokka**	national flower

一 十 艹 芢 芢 花 花 花

花 花

	ON readings リン **RIN** KUN readings はやし **hayashi**	meaning woods	8 strokes
			radical 木

林

common words

雑木林	ぞうきばやし	**zōkibayashi**	thicket of miscellaneous trees
林間学校	りんかんがっこう	**rinkan gakkō**	outdoor school
山林	さんりん	**sanrin**	forest land
竹林	ちくりん	**chikurin**	bamboo grove
林業	りんぎょう	**ringyō**	forestry
林道	りんどう	**rindō**	forest road

一　十　オ　木　木　杜　材　林

林　林　林

	ON readings シン **SHIN** KUN readings もり **mori**		meanings forest, grove		12 strokes radical 木

森

common words

森林	しんりん	**shinrin**	forest
森林公園	しんりんこうえん	**shinrinkōen**	forest park
森林浴	しんりんよく	**shinrin'yoku**	enjoying the scent of the woods, being invigorated by nature

一	十	才	木	朩	朩	朩	森
森	森	森	森	森	森	森	

	ON readings クウ **KŪ** **KUN readings** そら **sora**, あ-く **a-ku**, あ-ける **a-keru**, から **kara**	**meanings** sky; vacancy; emptiness	**8 strokes** **radical** 穴

空

common words

空っぽ(の)	からっぽ(の)	**karappo (no)**	empty
空気	くうき	**kūki**	air
空きカン	あきカン	**aki kan**	empty can
空手	からて	**karate**	karate
空席	くうせき	**kūseki**	vacant/unoccupied seat
航空便	こうくうびん	**kōkūbin**	airmail
空く	あく	**aku**	to become empty
空ける	あける	**akeru**	to vacate

ヽ¹	ʼʼ²	宀³	宀⁴	穴⁵	空⁶	空⁷	空⁸

空	空	空					

	ON readings カイ **KAI** KUN readings うみ **umi**		meanings sea, ocean	9 strokes radical 氵

海

common words

海辺	うみべ	**umibe**	seashore, seaside
海外	かいがい	**kaigai**	overseas, abroad
海岸	かいがん	**kaigan**	seacoast, seaside
海水浴	かいすいよく	**kaisuiyoku**	sea bathing
海水	かいすい	**kaisui**	sea water
海面	かいめん	**kaimen**	sea level
大海	たいかい	**taikai**	ocean

ON readings	meaning	9 strokes
シュン SHUN	spring	
KUN readings		**radical**
はる **haru**		日

春

common words

小春日和	こはるびより	**koharubiyori**	Indian summer
春夏秋冬	しゅんかしゅうとう	**shunkashūtō**	the four seasons
春分	しゅんぶん	**shunbun**	spring (vernal) equinox
青春	せいしゅん	**seishun**	adolescence
思春期	ししゅんき	**shishunki**	puberty
春休み	はるやすみ	**haruyasumi**	spring vacation
新春	しんしゅん	**shinshun**	the New Year

一 二 三 丰 夫 表 春 春

春 春 春 春

	ON readings カ **KA** KUN readings なつ **natsu**		meaning summer	10 strokes
夏	**common words** 初夏　　しょか　　　　**shoka**　　　　early summer 夏場　　なつば　　　　**natsuba**　　　summertime 夏休み　なつやすみ　　**natsuyasumi**　summer vacation 真夏　　まなつ　　　　**manatsu**　　　midsummer 夏期　　かき　　　　　**kaki**　　　　　summer period 夏物　　なつもの　　　**natsumono**　　summer clothing			radical 夂

一	丁	丆	百	百	百	百	頁
夏	夏	夏	夏	夏			

	ON readings シュウ **SHŪ** KUN readings あき **aki**	meanings fall, autumn	9 strokes
			radical 禾

秋

common words

秋風	あきかぜ	**akikaze**	autumn breeze
秋雨	あきさめ	**akisame**	autumnal rain
秋分の日	しゅうぶんのひ	**shūbun-no-hi**	Autumnal Equinox Day
初秋	しょしゅう	**shoshū**	early autumn
秋晴れ	あきばれ	**akibare**	fine autumn weather
晩秋	ばんしゅう	**banshū**	late autumn

	ON readings トウ **TŌ** KUN readings ふゆ **fuyu**		meaning winter	5 strokes
				radical 冬

冬

common words

冬眠	とうみん	**tōmin**	hibernation
冬物	ふゆもの	**fuyumono**	winter goods
冬休み	ふゆやすみ	**fuyuyasumi**	winter holidays
真冬	まふゆ	**mafuyu**	midwinter
冬空	ふゆぞら	**fuyuzora**	winter sky
冬期	とうき	**tōki**	winter period

ノ	ク	冬	冬	冬	冬	冬	冬
1	2	3	4	5			

	ON readings テン **TEN** **KUN readings** あめ **ame**, あま **ama**	**meanings** sky, heaven	**4 strokes** **radical** 大

天

common words

天の川	あまのがわ	**Amanogawa**	The Milky Way
天才	てんさい	**tensai**	genius
天使	てんし	**tenshi**	angel
天然	てんねん	**ten'nen**	nature
天下	てんか	**tenka**	the world
天気予報	てんきよほう	**tenkiyohō**	weather forecast
天国	てんごく	**tengoku**	paradise

一　二　天　天　天　天　天

	ON readings キ KI, ケ KE KUN readings		meanings spirit, energy, mind	6 strokes
				radical 气

気

common words

気分	きぶん	**kibun**	feeling
元気な	げんきな	**genki na**	energetic
天気	てんき	**tenki**	weather
病気	びょうき	**byōki**	sickness
気持(ち)	きもち	**kimochi**	feeling
気体	きたい	**kitai**	gaseous body, gas
人気	にんき	**ninki**	popularity
電気	でんき	**denki**	electricity

ノ₁	仁₂	仁₃	气₄	気	気₆	気	気
気							

ON readings ウ U KUN readings あめ **ame**, あま **ama**	meaning rain	8 strokes
		radical 雨

雨

common words

雨だれ	あまだれ	**amadare**	raindrop
雨ふり	あめふり	**amefuri**	rainy weather
小雨	こさめ	**kosame**	drizzle
にわか雨	にわかあめ	**niwaka ame**	sudden rain, shower
雨期	うき	**uki**	rainy season
雨天	うてん	**uten**	rainy weather
大雨	おおあめ	**ō'ame**	heavy rain
梅雨	つゆ	**tsuyu**	rainy season

一 厂 冂 币 雨 雨 雨 雨

雨 雨 雨

	ON readings セツ SETSU **KUN readings** ゆき yuki	**meaning** snow	**11 strokes** **radical** 雨

雪

common words

大雪	おおゆき	**ōyuki**	heavy snow
粉雪	こなゆき	**konayuki**	powder snow
雪景色	ゆきげしき	**yukigeshiki**	snowscape
雪だるま	ゆきだるま	**yukidaruma**	snowman
初雪	はつゆき	**hatsuyuki**	the first snow
新雪	しんせつ	**shinsetsu**	new-fallen snow

ON readings セイ **SEI** KUN readings は‐れ **ha-re**, は‐れる **ha-reru**, は‐らす **ha-rasu**	meanings fine weather; to clear	12 strokes radical 日

晴

common words

気晴らし	きばらし	**kibarashi**	amusement
晴天	せいてん	**seiten**	fine weather
晴れ着	はれぎ	**haregi**	one's best clothes
快晴	かいせい	**kaisei**	clear (weather)
晴れ	はれ	**hare**	fine (weather)
晴れる	はれる	**hareru**	to clear (weather), to be dispelled
晴らす	はらす	**harasu**	to dispel (doubts)

丨	冂	日	日	日	日	日	日
晴	晴	晴	晴	晴	晴	晴	

ON readings フウ **FŪ** **KUN readings** かぜ **kaze**		**meanings** wind; style	**9 strokes** **radical** 風

風

common words

風車	かざぐるま；ふうしゃ	**kazaguruma; fūsha**	pinwheel; windmill
強風	きょうふう	**kyōfū**	strong wind
台風	たいふう	**taifū**	typhoon
風景	ふうけい	**fūkei**	landscape
風邪	かぜ	**kaze**	a cold
風呂場	ふろば	**furoba**	bathroom
洋風	ようふう	**yōfū**	Western style
和風	わふう	**wafū**	Japanese style

丿 凡 凡 凡 凡 凨 凬 風

風 風 風 風

	ON readings シャ SHA KUN readings くるま kuruma		meanings wheel, vehicle, car	7 strokes
車	**common words** 自転車　　　じてんしゃ　　**jitensha**　　　bicycle 自動車　　　じどうしゃ　　**jidōsha**　　　automobile, car 歯車　　　　はぐるま　　　**haguruma**　　　gear 車体　　　　しゃたい　　　**shatai**　　　　body (automobile, vehicle) 下車する　　げしゃする　　**gesha suru**　　to get off (a train/car) 車内　　　　しゃない　　　**shanai**　　　　the inside of a car/train 電車　　　　でんしゃ　　　**densha**　　　　train			radical 車

ㄧ	厂	冂	戸	亘	車	車	車
車	車						

Radical Index

Japanese—English Index

I

MAI マイ 妹 younger sister 58
maiasa まいあさ 毎朝 every morning 42
maiban まいばん 毎晩 every night 41
maikai まいかい 毎回 every time 41
mainen まいねん 毎年 every year 41
mainichi まいにち 毎日 every day 41
maishoku まいしょく 毎食 each/every meal 41
maishū まいしゅう 毎週 every week 41
maitoshi まいとし 毎年 every year 41
maitsuki まいつき 毎月 every month 41
makka na まっかな 真っ赤な bright/clear red, crimson 84
makkuro na まっくろな 真っ黒な inky-black, jet-black 87
MAN マン 万 ten thousand 22
manatsu まなつ 真夏 midsummer 100
mangetsu まんげつ 満月 full moon 30
man'nenhitsu まんねんひつ 万年筆 fountain pen 22
manzoku まんぞく 満足 satisfaction 65
marugao まるがお 丸顔 round face 68
marui まるい 円い circular, round 23
massao まっさお 真っ青 paleness 85
mawaru まわる 回る go around 25
mawasu まわす 回す to turn 25
me め 女 woman, female 50
me め 目 eye 64
mejirushi めじるし 目印 mark 64
meshita めした 目下 one's subordinate 64
meue めうえ 目上 one's superior 64
mi み 三 three 12
migi みぎ 右 right 71
migigawa みぎがわ 右側 right side 71
migite みぎて 右手 right hand 71
migiude みぎうで 右腕 right arm, right-hand person 71
mikka みっか 三日 three days, 3rd day of the month 12
mikkabun みっかぶん 三日分 three days' worth 39
mikkakan みっかかん 三日間 (for) three days 48
mimi みみ 耳 ear 69
mimiate みみあて 耳あて earmuffs 69
mimi ga tōi みみがとおい 耳が遠い hard of hearing, deaf 69
mimikaki みみかき 耳かき earpick 69
mimikazari みみかざり 耳飾り earring 69
miminari みみなり 耳鳴り ringing in the ears 69
mimitabu みみたぶ 耳たぶ ear lobe 69
mimiuchi みみうち 耳打ち whispering 69
minami みなみ 南 south 82
Minami Amerika みなみアメリカ 南アメリカ South America 82
minamiguchi みなみぐち 南口 south exit/gate 82
minamikaze みなみかぜ 南風 south wind 82
mi(t)tsu み(っ)つ 三つ three (pieces; age) 12
miyage みやげ 土産 souvenir, gift 35
mizu みず 水 water 32

mizuiro みずいろ 水色 color of the sea 32
MOKU モク 木 tree, wood 33
MOKU モク 目 eye 64
mokuji もくじ 目次 table of contents 64
mokusei もくせい 木製 made of wood, wooden 33
mokuteki もくてき 目的 purpose 64
Mokuyōbi もくようび 木曜日 Thursday 36
mokuzai もくざい 木材 lumber, wood 33
mokuzō もくぞう 木造 wooden, made of wood 33
montei もんてい 門弟 follower 56
mori もり 森 forest, grove 96
moto もと 下 bottom, under 76
mu む 六 six 15
mucha na むちゃな 無茶な impossible 86
muika むいか 六日 six days, 6th day of the month 15
musuko むすこ 息子 son 54
musū (no) むすう(の) 無数(の) numerous 28
mu(t)tsu む(っ)つ 六つ six (pieces; age) 15

N

NAI ナイ 内 inside; home; within; between 77
naika ないか 内科 internal medicine unit; internal medicine 77
naiyō ないよう 内容 contents 77
naka なか 中 middle; within; inside 75
nakaba なかば 半ば middle, halfway 40
nakama なかま 仲間 partner, friend 48
nan なん 何 what, how many 45
NAN ナン 男 man, male 49
NAN ナン 南 south 82
nana なな 七 seven 16
nanahyaku ななひゃく 七百 seven hundred 16
nanaman'en ななまんえん 七万円 seventy thousand yen 16
nananin ななにん 七人 seven people 16
nanatsu ななつ 七つ seven (pieces; age) 16
Nanbei なんべい 南米 South America 82
nanbyaku なんびゃく 何百 how many hundreds; hundreds of ~ 20
nangatsu なんがつ 何月 what month 45
nangoku なんごく 南国 southern provinces/country 82
nani なに 何 what, how many 45
nanji なんじ 何時 what time 45
nanjikan なんじかん 何時間 how many hours 45
nankai なんかい 何回 how many times 45
Nankyoku なんきょく 南極 South Pole 82
nan'nen なんねん 何年 what year 45
nan'nichi なんにち 何日 what day 45
nan'nichikan なんにちかん 何日間 how many days 48
nan'nin なんにん 何人 how many people 45
nanoka なのか 七日 seven days, 7th day of the month 16
nanpun なんぷん 何分 how many minutes 45

SAN サン 山 mountain 90
sanbyaku さんびゃく 三百 three hundred 20
Sangatsu さんがつ 三月 March 12
sanji さんじ 三時 three o'clock 12
sanjū さんじゅう 三十 thirty 12
sankaku さんかく 三角 triangle 12
san'nen さんねん 三年 three years, the third year 12
san'nin さんにん 三人 three people 12
sanrin さんりん 山林 forest land 95
sanzen さんぜん 三千 three thousand 21
sasetsu kinshi させつきんし 左折禁止 No Left Turn 70
sayū さゆう 左右 left and right 70
SEI セイ 西 west 80
SEI セイ 青 blue; green; inexperienced 85
SEI セイ 晴 fine weather 107
seibu せいぶ 西部 western district/part 80
seibun せいぶん 成分 ingredient, component 39
seika せいか 聖火 sacred fire, Olympic torch 31
seinen せいねん 青年 youth 85
seinengappi せいねんがっぴ 生年月日 date of birth 30
seireki せいれき 西暦 the dominical year (A.D.) 80
seishōnen せいしょうねん 青少年 youth 85
seishun せいしゅん 青春 adolescence 99
seiten せいてん 晴天 fine weather 107
seiyō せいよう 西洋 the West, the Occident 80
SEKI セキ 赤 red 84
SEKI セキ 石 stone 93
sekidō せきどう 赤道 equator 84
sekijūji せきじゅうじ 赤十字 Red Cross 84
sekimen せきめん 赤面 blush 84
sekitan せきたん 石炭 coal 93
sekitei せきてい 石庭 stone garden 93
sekiyu せきゆ 石油 oil 93
sekken せっけん 石けん soap 93
SEN セン 千 thousand 21
SEN セン 川 river, stream 89
sen'en せんえん 千円 one thousand yen 21
sengetsu せんげつ 先月 last month 30
sen'nin せんにん 千人 one thousand people 21
senshu せんしゅ 選手 athlete 62
senshū せんしゅう 先週 last week 26
sentō せんとう 先頭 top, leader, head 67
sen'yū せんゆう 戦友 comrades in arms 60
SETSU セツ 雪 snow 106
SHA シャ 車 wheel, vehicle, car 109
SHAKU シャク 赤 red 84
SHAKU シャク 石 stone 93
shanai しゃない 車内 the inside of a car/train 109
shatai しゃたい 車体 body (automobile, vehicle) 109
SHI シ 四 four 13
SHI シ 子 child 54
SHI シ 姉 elder sister 57
SHI シ 私 private 59

shibutsu しぶつ 私物 private property 59
SHICHI シチ 七 seven 16
shichigatsu しちがつ 七月 July 16
shichiji しちじ 七時 seven o'clock 16
shichinin しちにん 七人 seven people 16
shifuku しふく 私服 plain/private clothes 59
Shigatsu しがつ 四月 April 13
shikaku しかく 四角 square 13
SHIKI シキ 色 color 88
shikisai しきさい 色彩 color, hue 88
shikishi しきし 色紙 square piece of fancy paper 88
shimai しまい 姉妹 sisters 58
shimo しも 下 bottom, under, beneath 76
SHIN シン 親 parent 53
SHIN シン 心 spirit, heart, mind 63
SHIN シン 森 forest, grove 96
shinai しない 市内 inside a city, civic 77
shingao しんがお 新顔 newcomer 68
shin'nichi しんにち 親日 pro-Japanese 53
shinpai しんぱい 心配 worry, anxiety 63
shinpu しんぷ 神父 (Christian) priest, father 51
shinrin しんりん 森林 forest 96
shinrinkōen しんりんこうえん 森林公園 forest park 96
shinrin'yoku しんりんよく 森林浴 enjoying the scents of the woods; being invigorated by 96
shinrui しんるい 親類 relative 53
shinsetsu しんせつ 新雪 new-fallen snow 106
shinsetsu na しんせつな 親切な kindly, friendly 53
shinshin しんしん 身心 body and mind 63
shinshun しんしゅん 新春 the New Year 99
shin'ya しんや 深夜 late-evening 44
shin'yū しんゆう 親友 close friend 60
shinzō しんぞう 心ぞう heart 63
shiritsu しりつ 私立 private (institution) 59
shiro しろ 白 white 83
shiroi しろい 白い white 83
shirokuro しろくろ 白黒 black-and-white 87
shiseikatsu しせいかつ 私生活 private life 59
shishobako ししょばこ 私書箱 P.O. Box 59
shishunki ししゅんき 思春期 puberty 99
shita した 下 bottom, under 76
shitagi したぎ 下着 underwear 76
shitamachi したまち 下町 downtown 76
shitashii したしい 親しい familiar 53
shitashimu したしむ 親しむ get familiar with 53
shitei してい 子弟 sons, children 56
shitei してい 姉弟 sister and brother 57
shitetsu してつ 私鉄 private railway 59
shiyō しよう 私用 private engagement 59
shiyōchū しようちゅう 使用中 in use, occupied 75
SHŌ ショウ 上 top, above, on 74
SHŌ ショウ 青 blue; green; inexperienced 85
shōgo しょうご 正午 noon 37
shōjo しょうじょ 少女 girl, maiden 50
shoka しょか 初夏 early summer 100

English–Japanese Index

colored pencil iroenpitsu 色えんぴつ 88

color of the sea mizu iro 水色 32

color up akarameru 赤らめる 84

coming from outside gairai 外来 78

commission tesūryō 手数料 62

complexion kaoiro 顔色 68

component seibun 成分 39

comrades in arms sen'yū 戦友 60

concentration shūchū 集中 75

concern kanshin 関心 63

confer kudasu 下す 76

contents naiyō 内容 77

context zengo 前後 72

core chūshin 中心 63

count kazoeru 数える 28

countenance kaodachi 顔立ち 68

countenance kaotsuki 顔付 68

counter for footwear SOKU 足 65

country (*national*) kokudo 国土 35

countryside inaka 田舎 92

coupon ticket kaisūken 回数券 25

course subject kamoku 科目 64

crimson makka na 真っ赤な 84

D

darkness ankoku 暗黒 87

date and time, the nichiji 日時 46

date of birth seinengappi 生年月日 30

dawn yoake 夜明け 44

day JITSU, NICHI, hi, ka 日 29

day (*counting*) NICHI 日 29

day, a ichi nichi 一日 10

day off kyūjitsu 休日 29

days of the week YŌ 曜 36

daytime CHŪ, hiru 昼 43

daytime hiruma 昼間 43

December Jūnigatsu 十二月 19

defeat haiboku 敗北 79

deficit akaji 赤字 84

descend oriru 下りる 76

descent kudari 下り 76

diplomacy gaikō 外交 78

disapproval nanshoku 難色 88

disciple deshi 弟子 56

dispel (*doubts*) harasu 晴らす 107

divide BUN, FUN 分 39

divide wakeru 分ける 39

domestic kokunai 国内 77

dominical year, the (A.D.) seireki 西暦 80

down kudari 下り 76

downstream kawashimo 川下 89

downtown shitamachi 下町 76

drizzle kosame 小雨 106

duty zeikin 税金 34

E

each MAI 毎 41

each meal maishoku 毎食 41

ear JI, mimi 耳 69

ear lobe mimitabu 耳たぶ 69

early autumn shoshū 初秋 101

early summer shoka 初夏 100

earmuffs mimiate 耳あて 69

earpick mimikaki 耳かき 69

earring mimikazari 耳飾り 69

earth DO, TO, tsuchi 土 35

ease of mind anshin 安心 63

east TŌ, higashi 東 81

east, west, south and north tōzainanboku 東西南北 81

east and west tōzai 東西 80

east exit/gate higashiguchi 東口 81

east side higashigawa 東側 81

East, the Orient, the Tōyō 東洋 81

eight HACHI, ya 八 17

eight (*pieces; age*) ya(t)tsu 八つ 17

eight days yōka 八日 17

eighth (8th) day (of the month), the yōka 八日 17

eight hundred happyaku 八百 17

eight o'clock hachiji 八時 17

eighty hachijū 八十 17

eight years hachinen 八年 17

elder toshiue no 年上の 74

elder brother KEI, KYŌ, ani 兄 55

elder brother oniisan お兄さん 55

elder brother (*familiar*) aniki 兄貴 55

elder sister SHI, ane 姉 57

elder sister onēsan お姉さん 57

elder sister (*polite*) ane'ue 姉上 57

eldest sister chōshi 長姉 57

eldest son chōnan 長男 49

electricity denki 電気 104

eleven jūichi 十一 19

emptiness KŪ, kara 空 97

empty karappo (no) 空っぽ(の) 97

empty can akikan 空きカン 97

energetic genki na 元気な 104

energy KE, KI 気 104

enjoying the scent of the woods shirin'yoku 森林浴 96

entrance iriguchi 入口 61

equator sekidō 赤道 84

era jidai 時代 46

evening YA, yo, yoru 夜 44

every MAI 毎 41

everybody banjin, ban'nin 万人 22

every day mainichi 毎日 41

every meal maishoku 毎食 41

every month maitsuki 毎月 41

every morning maiasa 今朝 42

every night maiban 毎晩 41

everyone banjin, ban'nin 万人 22

every time maikai 毎回 41

every week maishū 毎週 41

every year mainen, maitoshi 毎年 41

excursion ensoku 遠足 65

exit deguchi 出口 61

experience taiken 体験 66

explosion funka ふん火 31

eye BOKU, MOKU, ma, me 目 64

F

face GAN, kao 顔 68

face ganmen 顔面 68

face kaotsuki 顔付 68

fall SHŪ, aki 秋 101

familiar shitashii 親しい 53

father FU, chichi 父 51

father chichioya 父親 51

father otōsan お父さん 51

father (*Christian*) shinpu 神父 51

father (*polite*) chichiue 父上 51

father and mother fubo 父母 51

father-in-law gifu 義父 51

February Nigatsu 二月 11

fee tesūryō 手数料 62

feeling kibun 気分 104

feeling kimochi 気持(ち) 104

female JO, NYO, NYŌ, me, on'na 女 50

female josei 女性 50

female parent hahaoya 母親 52

field nohara 野原 91

field YA, no 野 91

field (*of endeavor*) bun'ya 分野 91

fields and gardens den'en 田園 92

fifth (5th) day (of the month), the itsuka 五日 14

fifty gojū 五十 14

fifty yen gojūen 五十円 23

figure (*math*) sūji 数字 28

fine (*weather*) hare 晴れ 107

fine autumn weather akibare 秋晴れ 101

fine weather SEI, hare 晴 107

fine weather seiten 晴天 107

fire KA, hi, ho 火 31

fire kaji 火事 31

fireworks hanabi 花火 31

first day (of the month), the tsuitachi 一日 *10*
first day, the ichinichime 一日目 *64*
first half, the zenpan, zenhan 前半 *40*
first language bokokugo 母国語 *52*
first snow, the hatsuyuki 初雪 *106*
fiscal year nendo 年度 *24*
five GO, itsu 五 *14*
five (*pieces; age*) itsutsu 五つ *14*
five days itsuka 五日 *14*
five hundred gohyaku 五百 *14*
five o'clock goji 五時 *14*
five thousand gosen 五千 *14*
five thousand yen gosen'en 五千円 *21*
florist hanaya 花屋 *94*
flower KA, hana 花 *94*
flower shop hanaya 花屋 *94*
focus chūshin 中心 *63*
follower montei 門弟 *56*
foot SOKU, ashi 足 *65*
foreign GAI, GE, soto, hoka 外 *78*
foreign country (people) gaikoku(jin) 外国(人) *78*
forest SHIN, mori 森 *96*
forest shinrin 森林 *96*
forest land sanrin 山林 *95*
forest park shinrinkōen 森林公園 *96*
forest road rindō 林道 *95*
forestry ringyō 林業 *95*
for four months yonkagetsu 四か月 *13*
for three days mikkakan 三日間 *48*
for twenty days hatsuka 二十日 *11*
foundation dodai 土台 *35*
fountain funsui ふん水 *32*
fountain pen man'nenhitsu 万年筆 *22*
four SHI, yo, yon 四 *13*
four (*pieces; age*) yo(t)tsu 四(っ)つ *13*
four days yokka 四日 *13*
four minutes yonpun 四分 *39*
four o'clock yoji 四時 *13*
four people yonin 四人 *13*
four seasons shunkashūtō 春夏秋冬 *99*
four times yonkai 四回 *13*
fraction bunsū 分数 *28*
Friday Kin'yōbi 金曜日 *36*
friend nakama 仲間 *48*
friend tomodachi 友だち *60*
friend YŪ, tomo 友 *60*

friend yūjin 友人 *60*
friendly shinsetsu na 親切な *53*
friendship yūjō 友情 *60*
friendship yūkō 友好 *60*
from now kongo 今後 *38*
full moon mangetsu 満月 *30*
future kongo 今後 *38*
future gojitsu 後日 *73*

G

garden tree ueki 植木 *33*
gas kitai 気体 *104*
gaseous body kitai 気体 *104*
gear haguruma 歯車 *109*
gem hōseki 宝石 *93*
genius tensai 天才 *103*
get familiar with shitashimu 親しむ *53*
get off (*a train/car*) gesha suru 下車する *109*
gift miyage 土産 *35*
girl joshi 女子 *50*
girl on'nanoko 女の子 *50*
girl shōjo 少女 *50*
give kudasaru 下さる *76*
gloves tebukuro 手袋 *62*
go around mawaru 回る *25*
go down oriru 下りる *76*
go down kudaru 下る *76*
go out gaishutsu suru 外出する *78*
go up noboru 上ぼる *74*
gold KIN, KON 金 *34*
gold kin'iro 金色 *88*
golden color kin'iro 金色 *88*
gold medal kinmedaru 金メダル *34*
grandfather sofu 祖父 *51*
grandmother sobo 祖母 *52*
green aoi 青い *85*
green SEI, ao 青 *85*
green (traffic) light aoshingō 青信号 *85*
greenery aoba 青葉 *85*
green leaf aoba 青葉 *85*
green tea ryokucha 緑茶 *86*
ground tochi 土地 *35*
group, a dantai 団体 *66*
grove SHIN, mori 森 *96*
guardians fukei 父兄 *55*
guidance an'nai 案内 *77*
gymnasium tai'ikukan 体育館 *66*

H

half hanbun 半分 *40*
half HAN 半 *40*
half a day han'nichi 半日 *40*

half a year hantoshi 半年 *40*
Half Off! hangaku 半がく *40*
half past one ichijihan 一時半 *40*
half price hangaku 半がく *40*
half the number hansū 半数 *28*
halfway nakaba 半ば *40*
hammer kanazuchi 金づち *34*
hand SHU, te 手 *62*
handshake akushu 握手 *62*
hang sageru 下げる *76*
hang down sagaru 下がる *76*
hard of hearing mimi ga tōi 耳が遠い *69*
harmonious enman na 円満な *23*
hat bōshi 帽子 *54*
head sentō 先頭 *67*
head TO, TŌ, ZU, atama, kashira 頭 *67*
head zunō 頭脳 *67*
headache zutsū 頭痛 *67*
head teacher kyōtō 教頭 *67*
heap(ing) yamamori (no) 山盛り(の) *90*
heart SHIN, kokoro 心 *63*
heart shinzō 心ぞう *63*
heaven TEN, ama, ame 天 *103*
heavy rain ō'ame 大雨 *105*
heavy snow ōyuki 大雪 *106*
helter-skelter uōsaō 右往左往 *71*
hibernation tōmin 冬眠 *102*
high value of the yen endaka 円高 *23*
hills and fields noyama 野山 *91*
holiday kyūjitsu 休日 *29*
home DAI, NAI, uchi 内 *77*
horizontal suihei na 水平な *32*
hour JI, toki 時 *46*
hour jikan 時間 *46*
housetop okujō 屋上 *74*
how many KA, nan, nani 何 *45*
how many days nan'nichikan 何日間 *48*
how many hours nanjikan 何時間 *45*
how many hundreds nanbyaku 何百 *20*
how many minutes nanpun 何分 *45*
how many people nan'nin 何人 *45*
how many times nankai 何回 *45*
how many weeks nanshūkan 何週間 *48*
hue shikisai 色彩 *88*
human being ningen 人間 *48*
hundred HYAKU 百 *20*
hundred (trees, bottles or thin long things) hyappon 百本 *20*

within CHŪ, naka 中 75
within NAI, uchi 内 77
with shoes on dosoku 土足 65
woman JO, NYO, NYŌ, me,
   on'na 女 50
woman joshi 女子 50
women's college joshidai 女子大 50
women's university joshidai 女子
   大 50
wood MOKU, ki 木 33
wood mokuzai 木材 33
wooden mokusei 木製 33
wooden mokuzō 木造 33
woods RIN, hayashi 林 95
world, the tenka 天下 103

worry shinpai 心配 63
woven wire kana-ami 金あみ 34

Y

Yamanote line Yamanote-sen 山手
   線 90
year NEN, toshi 年 24
year-end party bōnenkai 忘年会 24
years (days) ago, …
   nen (nichi) mae,… 〜年(日)前 72
years (days) after, …
   nen (nichi) go,… 〜年(日)後 73
yen (Japanese monetary unit) EN
   円 23
yesterday kinō, sakujitsu 昨日 73

young lady onēsan お姉さん 57
young male oniisan お兄さん 55
younger brother DAI, TEI,
   otōto 弟 56
younger brothers and sisters tei-
   mai 弟妹 56
younger sister MAI, imōto 妹 58
your younger brother
   (polite) otōtosan 弟さん 56
your younger sister
   (polite) imōtosan 妹さん 58
youth seinen 青年 85
youth seishōnen 青少年 85